The 7 D's to Your Destiny

Amy Burkett

ISBN: 978-1-7356580-0-1

The 7 D's to Your Destiny

CONTENT

ACKNOWLEDGMENTS

Thank you to:
Dominic Dezzutti, my editor;
Rob Upton, my photographer, graphic designer
and tech support team.

This book is dedicated to:

My heavenly father who has never left me and filled
every void left from not really knowing my earthly father.
To my grandfather who instilled in me that anything was possible.
To my mom who trained me in the way I should go and always
loved me.
To my husband Rob; what an amazing journey God has brought us
on. Thank you for all your support.
To my son RJ; I love you more than words can describe and I can't
wait to see what GOD does through YOU.

INTRODUCTION

Congratulations! Your life makes a difference for others and you're taking the steps to walk into your great destiny by reading this book. I know what you're thinking, "You don't know me, Amy." But, really, I do.

We all share a common bond to want to make a positive impact on this world. When we act on those positive desires, we make our world a better place. I am talking about the desire for our lives to matter to someone else, not the desire for a new car or a bigger house.

Author Steven Furtick said, "When you attach your significance to status and your security to things, it's never enough." I love that quote, because it sums up a huge part of our culture these days.

I've believed for most of my adult life that I had a greater assignment than just existing. You know what I mean. Getting up, going to work, taking care of the family, then going to bed exhausted and doing it all over again tomorrow, and the next day and the day after. Do you feel sometimes like you're trapped in the movie Groundhog Day?

Now don't get me wrong, life has a certain repetitive nature to it. However, the question is this, "What *should* you be repeating every day and what *should* you stop doing right now?"

What do you want your life to look like? How do you want to live it? Where do you want to have a positive impact?

I want to help you answer those questions for yourself in this book. I want to help you fight past the superficial desire for status and things and help you create a more meaningful, satisfying life by sharing the seven D's to your true destiny.

"Destiny is not a matter of chance; it is a matter of choice. It is not a thing to be waited for, it is a thing to be achieved."
— William Jennings Bryan

You have the power and ability to create the life you've always dreamed about. The question is do you have the discipline required to live the life you were created to live? Discipline is one of those critical D's necessary for you to walk into your great destiny, but more on that later.

Life is full of so many questions. Leadership guru and New York Times bestselling author John Maxwell said, "Most people spend more time planning their vacations, than they do planning their lives." Ouch, that hurts. I used to be one of those people, and to be honest from time to time I still struggle, but I'm much more intentional about life these days. I think you want to be more intentional with your life too, because you're taking the time to invest in yourself right now. Let's learn to be more intentional together!

Intentionality is an important building block for creating your best life. Make one intentional act and keep doing it until it becomes a natural part of your life, then start another. I'll talk a lot about John Maxwell throughout this book, because his writing has been the catalyst for change in my life and I'm so very grateful to call him my mentor and friend. Details on that later too. His destiny of being a leadership author, put me on the path to finding my destiny.

My life changed for the better in 1999. After nine years chasing plane crashes and hostage ordeals as a commercial television news anchor and reporter, at the age of 31, I had accepted a new job as executive producer of a PBS station in Bethlehem, Pennsylvania. Spot news was behind me and stories of substance were in my future.

Now, I say my life changed for the better, but it was the beginning of a crazy rollercoaster of stress, problems and possibilities. Why would anyone consider that to be a great step in their lives? Well, I woke up and I became intentional about my personal growth. Most people are unwilling to invest in themselves.

The greatest investment you can make is investing in personal growth. You can't give to others what you don't have in yourself. Everybody has the ability to do this. It doesn't require any special talent, just discipline and desire. There I go again getting ahead of myself and talking about future chapters. It'll all make sense in a bit, I promise.

I hope the words throughout this book will stir your soul. If you let it intentionally work to develop the 7 D's to your Destiny, you'll be living the life you were created to enjoy and will be fulfilling your purpose. Why would you settle for anything less?

"You are not the victim of the world, but rather the master of your own destiny. It is your choices and decisions that determine your destiny."
— Roy T. Bennett

I think an important part of life is realizing we're all a work in progress. Evangelist Billy Graham's wife Ruth used to always say she was "under construction." I love that phrase. Don't you? On Ruth Graham's tombstone, which I've seen in the courtyard of the Billy Graham Library in Charlotte, North Carolina, it reads, "Construction Complete." We're all under construction until we take our last breath and since we haven't done that yet, let's keep working on ourselves!

A part of me that has been a work in progress is becoming an author. I have always been a writer. I started writing puppet plays in the first grade. My friend Angie Farrell drew the puppets. I went on to win essay contests in the third grade and beyond. About a decade ago, I started having the feeling I should write a book, but I didn't have any idea what I'd write about.

I used to serve as a National Trustee for the National Academy of Television Arts and Sciences, the organization that plans the "Daytime Emmy Awards." At a Trustee meeting, I told my long-time friend, Dominic Dezzutti about my concept for a book.

My idea was about my first assertive act in the second grade, which was to walk down a long and winding path at Busch Gardens in Florida to ride an elephant. My single mom and teenage sisters wanted to browse the gift shops. My mom told me that if I wanted to wait in the line to ride the elephant to go ahead, but the three of them would be shopping. My sisters told me they'd leave me. I was terrified that my sisters would actually leave, but I was pretty sure my mom wouldn't let them. This was our first family vacation. The end of the story was my mom didn't leave me, and I rode that elephant, and that ride changed everything. It set in motion everything else in my life that needed courage in the face of doubt.

Dominic and I were excited about the book idea and we stayed up until the wee hours of the morning brainstorming ideas for it. He has all the good ideas for clever elephant related chapter titles during that late night conversation that supported the title, "Ride Your Elephant."

I spent months forcing myself to fill in the details, but it was awful. The book was turning out to be too much about me. It seemed like a very dull memoir and wasn't doing enough to help others, so I scratched it, literally, I deleted it, but I learned a lot through the process.

Another five years passed in the blink of an eye. In the fall of 2017, as the General Manager of WTVI PBS Charlotte, I created a seven week career pathways and leadership program to be taught in two of the poorest high schools in Charlotte.

As beautiful and shiny as Charlotte, North Carolina looks to visitors, it's a tale of two cities. One Charlotte is a prosperous, rapidly growing business hub. The other landed dead last on a Harvard University study ranking cities on existing opportunities for people to pull themselves out of poverty.

I wanted to use the power of media and my leadership experience to help inner city high school students break that cycle of poverty by exposing them to career pathways and equipping them with leadership principles that could change their lives for the better.

Over the course of the class, students write and record, on camera, their own, "I Have a Dream," speeches. It's a powerful thing when young people declare what their dreams are. I felt compelled to try to empower these disadvantaged, but terrific teens who I saw full of possibilities and potential.

Fast forward to our first graduating class. I needed to write words that I hoped would encourage them. The program was called the 3D project: Dreamers-Doers-Destiny.

In my first graduation speech to them, I created a few tips I called the 7 D's to Your Destiny to help them find their destiny and this book found me that day. These terrific teens are so incredibly resilient. Teens like Shemiah, whose dad went to prison when she was two. Her life has been tougher than most can imagine, but her smile lights up a room. She was sexually assaulted, but even turned that into a positive by creating a club at her school focused on preventing others from going through what she had endured. I had the pleasure of having her in my class her senior year. The day she graduated from our program is the day her dad got out of prison.

At the end of this book, I'll share more stories from my students about their dreams and the feedback they've given me about the impact the program had on them.

The big difference between my two book writing efforts was the first one was about me simply wanting to write a book and this effort that you are reading right now is about me using my life experiences to help others fulfill their life's purpose and find their destiny. We should always focus on others and I know it's not always easy, but it's always rewarding.

"The high destiny of the individual is to serve rather than to rule." Albert Einstein

I know first hand how hard it can be to keep your focus on others, but when we do, the results are so much better and so much more satisfying. I have been compelled to write this book over the last three years. The words just flowed out of my fingertips...that is when I actually had the discipline to sit down and write.

Before I give the whole book away, let's just dive in. We'll start pulling back the onion layers to learn more strategies of the 7 D's to Your Destiny. These principles can help lead YOU toward YOUR great destiny, because each of us was created for GREATNESS!

CHAPTER 1
DESIRE DEFINES YOUR DREAM

"The starting point of all achievement is desire."
Napoleon Hill

What do you desire? It sounds like an easy question, but it's tricky. The older I get, I think the trickier it gets to define. When I graduated college, I desired success. It wasn't about what I could give the world, it was about what the world could give me. I'm not proud of that, but I'm always going to be honest and transparent with you. Perhaps you can relate to that feeling.

Desire is your fuel. It powers your dreams and helps you push through the challenges of life. I know you have challenges. We all do. However, I find it hard to imagine that your only desire is to arrive successfully at death without accomplishing anything meaningful along the way.

I'm pretty sure you want more out of life, but you just don't know how to get there from where you are now. The first step is to learn how to tap into your desire. Actually it's a little harder than that. You need to tap into the right kind of desire, which rarely focuses on you and is almost always about how you can make a positive impact on others.

"Men go far greater to avoid what they fear than to obtain what they desire." Dan Brown, The Da Vinci Code

Let me elaborate on the different kinds of desire and how one kind can be helpful and the other can lead you down the wrong path.

I graduated with a Bachelor of Science degree in Journalism and spent nine years in commercial television, singularly focused on me and trying to become a better television anchor and reporter. I loved writing and adored being around people, so this was a great career fit for me. It was at the intersection of my passion and talents.

What I didn't know was just how difficult being on television was for your self-esteem. I heard it all. I wasn't pretty enough, talented enough, or thin enough to be successful as on-air talent. Consultants told me I didn't have "IT." They couldn't define what "IT" was, but they knew I didn't have it.

My first job out of college was at a tiny NBC affiliate in Zanesville, Ohio. There are 210 television markets in the United States, with cities ranked by population from largest to smallest. New York City is number one. Zanesville, back in 1990, was number 198. I couldn't have started much lower, but I felt there was nowhere to go but up from there.

In commercial television, I pushed to get great TV assignments like covering plane crashes, hurricanes and hostage ordeals. I know it sounds a little twisted to consider those things great assignments, but that's too often the mindset of many TV news reporters. It only takes covering one horrible disaster to launch your career and get you to a larger market or the network, which is the goal for so many. That's where my wrong headed desire got me early in my career.

If you're in a place right now whether it's in your career or your studies, and you are focused on yourself, fear not! That focus doesn't mean you've lost your way, because it's often part of the process. Working in commercial television pulled my focus in two directions. One was just about me strengthening my skills and the other was about me sharing the stories of the extraordinary people I got to interview every day. Everyone has a story to tell and I loved getting to know them and crafting their life into meaningful words and visuals that allowed them to shine. Human interest stories were always my favorite. As I look back on those early years of just focusing on me, my motives were wrong, but the process was right. I had to get better. My writing, voice, presentation skills, it all needed improving for sure. If I hadn't accomplished those improvements, I wouldn't have been able to help others do the same.

When I finally made the move to public television, it was a move that spoke to my soul and was fueled by my desire to do more for others and more specifically, I desired to lead and serve others. Now that I was at a local PBS station and I created television content that educated, inspired and entertained, I was one step closer to my destiny. I desired greatness for my team, our community and when I accomplished that I would also find my greatness.

A key element to remember is that desire is the critical fuel for the first step toward your dream, because those first steps can be the toughest. One of the many things I didn't know about leading a team was how to motivate the group. I inherited a team of people in a television station where everybody, except me, seemed to know that station's reputation at the time, was "a place good careers go to die." When someone at a local commercial station told me that after I had started, I was shocked.

Here's a really important clarifying statement for new leaders, if your team doesn't want you to succeed, they will most likely help you fail. I had every problem under the sun with that original team. First, they tried to scare me away. The last Executive Producer only lasted about a month. They found every reason not to do what I was asking.

John Maxwell once wrote, "People have to know you care, before they care about your plan." Now it's one thing to say it and an entirely different thing to make it happen, my friends. I knew I needed them in order to create meaningful content for our community, but they weren't too excited about the changes I was suggesting.

I was naive to think that everyone would just do what I asked, because I was the boss. That was one of my first mistakes, seeing myself as the boss and not as the leader. I loved people and wanted them to love me too.

Yet another mistake of mine, wanting to be liked more than I wanted to lead.

Danger Will Robinson! This is a fatal flaw in leadership. Leaders aren't running popularity contests. Thank you, James Baum for teaching me that important point. James was the General Manager who hired me at the Pennsylvania PBS station.

What this team taught me was that as a leader I needed the courage to make the difficult decisions, no matter what, to move all of us forward.

Desire kicks back in when you hit tough times too. They become roadblocks to making your dream your reality.

Freedom to Dream

Hold on we've got to shift gears here. Now that you better understand how to recognize the right desires in your life, we need to figure out how to connect them to our dreams.

So let's go back and talk about that first team of mine in Pennsylvania. From my perspective, the team wasn't bad or untalented, but somewhere along the way they lost their desire or ability to dream, which is heartbreaking to me. They seemed to just want a paycheck to do things the way they had always done them. Maybe you can relate. You might feel all you need is a paycheck and want to just focus on the path of least resistance to get it. It's a choice so many make, because it's easy. However, it isn't fulfilling and it robs you of finding your great destiny.

What my team taught me was that they had lost the freedom to dream and I knew I needed to try and restore it for them. Many chose not to, but those I hired seemed to thrive that way. It was key for them and I want to help you find that freedom as well.

Difficult circumstances in all of our lives can rob us of our freedom to dream. We can lose the joy of life from the events that happen to us and we end up simply just trying to survive, and not realizing how dreaming can help us thrive. If this has happened to you, I want to restore your freedom to dream. Don't worry it's not too late. As long as you still have breath, you can do it.

Here are three steps to help give you the freedom to dream.

First, you must love yourself and others. Sometimes life has a way of beating us down, crushing our dreams and killing our desire. You may be tempted to give up on your dream. When you love yourself enough to change yourself, to grow into that dream achiever, you'll be on your way.

Second, listen to your inner voice and others who often recognize talents in us that we can't see. A family member or a friend may give you that little encouragement to remind you that you're capable of so much more. I call that a "jump start." You know when your car battery is dead and you need a jump to get it started. Sometimes our desire and dreams need a little jump start to get them firing again. Don't ignore that recurring inner nudge. That's your desire begging you to listen. Quiet yourself and truly listen to your heart's desire. Trust me, I know how difficult it is to quiet myself. I'm a type A personality who has one speed, fast.

Third, allow yourself to get excited about learning again. Learning things in your area of interest helps you define your desire and rekindles our ability to dream. When we learn, we expand our horizons, we gain new perspectives and all of this becomes the ingredients for the recipe to create the life we always hoped we could enjoy. Dreams need fuel to keep them going and learning is that special octane our dreams desire.

You've been holding your dreams hostage and it's time to free them. No matter what day or what month you're reading this, IT'S INDEPENDENCE DAY FOR YOUR DREAMS. Imagine the fireworks lighting up the night sky as they're bursting in air. How does that image make you feel? Savor the excitement. Absorb the joy. Let those images of bombs bursting in air with those vibrant colors sear into your memory. Don't let go of how it makes you feel and set out to create a plan to make your life that daily celebration.

Dream Tip: Be careful not to confuse a dream with a goal. Goals often become just another item on your to do list. Crossing things off a list can feel good, but it doesn't last for long. If it can be crossed off easily, then it's not a dream. Aim higher! Desire more!

"The stronger the desire, the greater the motivation. The stronger the motivation, the greater the achievement." Author Unknown

Defining Desire

Webster's dictionary defines desire as a strong wish or want. The type of desire necessary to propel you into your destiny is much stronger than that. It's an all consuming craving, or yearning, to accomplish your assignment in this world.

Failure is not an option.

That phrase has been the key to my desires and dreams for decades.

First, you must believe there is a way to accomplish what you're working toward. No matter how crazy the idea, or far away the finish line, you must believe there is a way to make it happen. Now, along the way, you will find failure. Trust me, you won't be able to truly define your desire until you figure out how to handle failing.

When I was a kid I loved playing with Legos and Lincoln Logs. I'd have some idea of what I wanted to build, but I'd be missing a key piece. You know what I mean...that odd shaped piece that the set didn't give you enough of to build your masterpiece.

Here's the thing. I could have simply accepted that my masterpiece could not exist because of my limited Legos set. But instead, I refused to accept that. I refused to accept failure. It is that refusal to give up that truly makes everything you want to achieve a reality.

Trust me, you will fail many times in your attempts in defining your desire, but that's ok and necessary. That's not really failure in my eyes that's stumbling and learning. An unsuccessful attempt shows you're learning and getting closer to making your dreams come true. The only real failure in life is not trying or giving up too soon. You have no idea how close you are to success, when you give up.

Often, the next exit on the highway of life is where you will find success and if you let the idea of failure stop you now, you would have pulled off just a mile too soon.

Don't do it my friends! You'll thank me later. Push through and keep trying.

Follow the wise advice of Dory in Disney's animated movie "Finding Nemo," and just keep swimming. Just keep swimming.

Now we've got to break down what it means to desire something. I'm not talking about the desire for things like a new outfit or pair of shoes. That's more of a "want" versus a desire, even in the best of sales.

What I'm talking about is an all-consuming desire, as if your life depends on it, because it does. Once you figure out your "why," that's when you can really start defining your desire and working toward your destiny. Don't miss that my friends. The real key to desire is understanding WHY you want it so badly.

Do you know your why? It took me a long time to put it into words, but here's a really good activity that can help you find it too. Write your personal mission statement. That is the ultimate answer to your why!

I know what you're saying right now. "Amy, I'm not a company. I don't need a mission statement. I'm just an individual."

Which word in that last sentence do you think is preventing you from completing the assignment? It's the word "JUST."

You are not "JUST" anything. In fact, you are an individual created for greatness. You were "fearfully and wonderfully made, "Psalm 139:14. You need to bond with that phrase and really believe it. Your great destiny is out there waiting for you, and OTHERS NEED YOU TO FIND IT! They're depending on YOU, because YOU'RE the key to them finding their great destiny. If you won't do it for yourself, do it for your family, friends, neighbors, coworkers, and all the other people just waiting to meet you, because you can help change their direction in life for the better.

Ok, back to the mission statement helping you define your why.

Here's my mission statement:

I was created to grow myself and others to be all we were created to be for the benefit of our communities and the glory of God.

If someone asks why I do something, anything that I feel is for the betterment of my team or my ability to lead them, this statement is the answer. It speaks to who I am at my core.

I'm a person of faith and that is a huge part of my why and what fuels my desire. I was raised in church and my grandmother was one of the biggest prayer warriors I've ever met. She prayed for hours every night. Sometimes I'd sit outside her door and just listen. Her faith encouraged me to develop my own relationship with Jesus.

I'm a Christian and I want you to know that I respect you and whatever faith you may or may not follow. I can't hide that following Jesus Christ is the best decision I've ever made and is the reason I've been able to accomplish so many of my dreams.

I'm so grateful my single mom and grandmother shared their faith with me, when I was a child. I've relied on it every day to help me fight for my dreams. My faith helps me define my why, which helps me to define my desire and that is what keeps pulling me back to living up to my potential.

But here's the thing, whatever your why is rooted in, whether it be your faith or something completely different, if you are focused on having a why that will help others, then you are on your way!

So, let's take a little time to have a writing lesson now. I want to help you craft that critical mission statement.

Step 1 Search company mission statements and look for examples that speak to your soul.

Here are a few that get my engine revving.

LinkedIn: "To connect the world's professionals to make them more productive and successful."

Facebook: "To give people the power to share and make the world more open and connected."

Sony: "To be a company that inspires and fulfils your curiosity."

Kickstarter "To help bring creative projects to life."

These are just four of my favorites, you'll need to research ones that speak to your desires.

What do all of these mission statements have in common? They all use strong action verbs, briefly make their point in 15 words or less and make me feel hopeful.

Step 2 Write something, anything, and then let it sit for a few days.

Step 3 Share it with a friend who knows you very well and will be honest and not just blow sunshine at you and tell you it's great. Ask them if it sounds like you.

Step 4 Edit your original statement and repeat steps 1-4 as many times as it takes until you've written something that will help you get up in the morning and face whatever the world throws at you. This should be a statement that you can easily memorize and proudly repeat to anyone you meet.

Unshakeable Desire

There is very likely something that you want to achieve, something you desire, but you keep finding reasons or in many cases excuses not to do it. You may try to write it off as some crazy idea, but I am here to tell you that it's not crazy.

I bet that this "DESIRE" is something you simply can't shake. Perhaps you've tried to avoid it. You may have been successful at writing it off for a month, a year or decades, but today is your day to pay attention to that little voice, that tiny burning ember that has never gone away. What I want to do is pour some gasoline on that little teeny tiny flicker inside you so it burns brighter and stronger and you can't ignore it any longer. When that tiny ember becomes an out of control wildfire, that's the kind of desire I am talking about.

Right now you might be saying, "But Amy, you don't understand my challenges. You don't understand the odds that are stacked against me."

People with desire overcome the odds every day. People like Althea Gibson. She was born in South Carolina back in 1927. She was the first black athlete to cross the color barrier and win a grand slam title in professional tennis when she won the French Open in 1956. She went on to win titles at Wimbledon and the U.S Nationals, which was the precursor to the U.S Open.

Althea Gibson is proof of the effectiveness of desire because there is no way she could have achieved what she did without wanting it more than anything else in the world. It would have been easy to think that her odds of winning were about a zillion-to-one, but she never believed that. She trained every day and her desire raged like an out of control bonfire. It was her desire that helped her beat the odds.

I never knew Althea Gibson, but I bet there were a lot of people that thought she couldn't achieve what she did. But she wisely chose to ignore the people who said it couldn't be done.

No one else needs to believe in your dream to make it come true, but if you don't believe in yourself, it will never happen. I learned that in one of John Maxwell's books. To me, failure only happens when you stop trying.

Althea didn't know she couldn't win, so she did. I think there's some Althea in you, begging to come out. If she could do it, you can too.

We all have desire, it's just so unfortunate how often we ignore it. We often let the pain of life sweep it under the rug. We tell ourselves we need to keep the reliable job that pays the bills, even though we hate it with a passion.

If you can relate to this feeling, hating your job but not knowing a way out, let's tackle this right now!

I'm not saying walk in and quit today, but what have you done to get a different job? If the answer is nothing, then that changes now.

The key step is to do something about it. What I want you to do right now is to take out your calendar and book yourself one hour tomorrow to actively look for a new job.

Don't just surf the internet, scouring job sites. Spend 30 minutes really looking, then spend 30 minutes applying for the one that excites you.

It may not be the perfect job, but at least you will be taking action toward getting out of your current situation. Action and desire go hand in hand and I'll talk about action a lot in this book. I promise that you'll feel better after taking action and even if you don't get it or it's not the perfect job, it can be the next step necessary to get you closer to the perfect job.

When you stop to really do something about your desire, it gives you a special feeling that nothing else can match. You might feel accomplished, satisfied, invigorated and maybe even a little scared. That's okay. That crazy energy that you are feeling is going to build to even greater satisfaction.

The thing about desire is the more steps you take toward fulfilling it, the more your desire burns and provides the fuel to help you take a few more steps. Once you nurture your desire enough, it becomes part of your DNA. True DNA desire is the greatest present, because it lasts forever. You may throw water on it, but it's still smoldering inside of you and taking action is the key. I'm here to help you build that kind of desire!

Let me take you back to1987, my freshman year in college at Bowling Green State University in Ohio. I knew I wanted to be a journalist since I was five when I would watch the nightly news with Walter Cronkite, sitting on my grandfather's lap. He said to me, "Buddy, you could do that one day." I decided right then that I would, but I had no idea how long it would take and how determined I would need to be to make it happen or how important my desire would be to keep me on track to pursuing it.

At BGSU, the journalism department mandated that incoming students take an entrance exam in the second semester freshman year. I failed my entrance to journalism test, not once, twice, or three times. It took me five tries to pass that ridiculous test..

I thought my career was over before it began, but my desire taught me a critical lesson. It wouldn't let me quit trying. Tenacity is a by-product of desire. They go hand in hand. My desire generated the tenacity I needed to keep taking that stupid test, which was the one thing standing between me and the road that would lead to my destiny. I don't think I'd ever heard the word tenacity before at that point in my life, but desire pushed me toward it every single day. I really never thought of quitting. It didn't seem like an option.

Unfortunately, my grandfather died when I was a sophomore in high school, so he wasn't around to encourage me to keep trying. But my grandfather used to always tell me, "If at first you don't succeed buddy, try, try again." It was the vision of the end result that kept me going, when I didn't "feel" like trying.

John Maxwell says, "Begin with the end in mind." Desire allows you to paint a picture of what your future could look like. Remember to paint a picture using as many details as possible. Chances are that it won't turn out exactly like you picture it, but it most likely will be even better. That vision, which is part of desire, will help you get to the next step. Every step gets you closer.

Desire is such a beautiful thing, but you've got to check your motives. Are your desires worth pursuing? How will they help others? If the only person who benefits from your desire is YOU, then you've got more work to do.

Another way to look at it is every step you take, even the wrong ones, will lead you closer to your destiny. That is if you follow your true inner desire. But who wants to take the long way? In the Bible the Israelites could have made it to the promised land in a couple weeks, but it took them 40 years. I'm afraid life often takes us the long way to our destiny. We wouldn't be able to handle it if we got there sooner. And our story wouldn't be as relatable and encouraging to others, if it were easy.

Desire's DNA

So how do you really understand what your true desire is and how do you differentiate it from the everyday wants or passing whims? Here's an exercise that can help.

Look back over your life and see what recurring themes you find. I had been a writer since childhood. I thought it was just a hobby for the longest time, but it would never really go away. I put it on the shelf many times, but that yearning to tell stories always came back. I also loved being around people. I liked encouraging them. I didn't realize I was doing it most of the time. It was just part of who I was.

It doesn't matter what age you are, your past is cluttered with desire clues that will help you define your dream and lead you to your destiny. From my perspective it's in your DNA. Look back to your childhood, teenage years, 20s, 30s, 40s what keeps drawing you back? Are you being pulled in a different direction than your current reality? Once you identify it, you're on your way.

As we wrap up our chapter on desire, my question is how badly do you want to tap into your destiny? Are you willing to go through the painful process of change? Are you willing to give up a little sleep to work on activating your desire to achieve your destiny? It seems like a fairly small price to pay to help you live the extraordinary life you were created to live, but only you can decide.

Remember the three steps to give you the freedom to dream so you can free your desire.

1. Love yourself enough to change yourself.
2. Listen to your inner voice.
3. Get excited about learning.

Have you written your personal mission statement? When you do, put it somewhere you can read it every day, until it just slides off your tongue effortlessly.

Let your desire pull you to achieve your dreams like Althea Gibson did.

It doesn't sound too difficult in theory, does it? But here's where things get tough, you need to change your habits and that's going to take you about 21 days. Get up an hour early every single morning for three weeks. Don't do it five days and take the weekends off. You've got to go all in and do it every day. Find a book related to what you see as a desire that keeps reoccurring and read it during that time.

Reading is a great, inexpensive, catalyst toward change. That hour you get when you wake up early every day can be like a treasure map cluttered with clues leading you to the desire that defines your GREAT destiny.

I'm so VERY proud of you. You've set the groundwork in this first chapter toward learning that DESIRE DEFINES YOUR DREAM.

The hardest part and the longest chapter in this book is now behind you. Congratulations, but don't stop here. Keep reading your destiny's waiting.

CHAPTER 2
DISCOVER YOUR PASSION

"Passion is energy. Feel the power that comes from focusing on what excites you." Oprah Winfrey

I need to take you back to 1999, when I was 31 and leading the production department at the PBS station in Pennsylvania. Sometimes in life you have to lose to win. I realize that seems counterintuitive, but I'm sure you have stories like this in your life.

I wasn't the winning candidate for that job the first time. I applied, interviewed and didn't get the job at the end of 1998.

I couldn't shake the feeling that I was meant to have that job. Sure, I was disappointed when I didn't get it, but I did a crazy thing that day. It was something I'd never done before. I praised GOD in my disappointment. I let my passion for my faith fill the void of my disappointment. It was a pivotal moment in my life.

I got on my treadmill, ran, cried and praised GOD for HIS plan. I thanked him for whatever HE had in store for me. I was honest and poured out my sadness and disappointment to the ultimate creator of my destiny.

The lesson here is showing gratitude during grief. Powerful things happen when you do that and discovering your passion is just one of them.

I had no idea how that would change the trajectory of my life. I learned how to actually praise HIM in the storm at that moment and it has served me so well ever since.

Every time I drove past the sign for the station, which was near where I lived, I felt like that job was coming back to me. I know it sounds crazy, but it was one of the strongest feelings I've ever had.

On New Year's Eve, I saw that the position I interviewed for had been reposted. I'll NEVER forget what I did next. I picked up the phone and called the station president. I didn't know exactly what I was going to say. He didn't pick up, but I got his voicemail and my passion took over.

I said, "Good morning sir, this is Amy Burkett, the candidate for Executive Producer that you didn't hire. I see the position is open again and I don't know if you just didn't like me or if I was your second choice, but I want to come and turn your station into an Emmy Award winning organization. If you're interested, please give me a call, if not, Happy New Year."

I hung up the phone and didn't know exactly what I'd done, but ten minutes later, he called and offered me the job. I asked him why he didn't let me know the position was open again. He said he didn't think I'd be interested after he didn't hire me the first time. WOW! It's hard for me to imagine what my life would have been like, if I hadn't made that call.

According to the website DailyMail.com, 74 percent of Americans have quit a job to pursue their passions. Passion may look a little different for everyone, but I see it as an intense enthusiasm for something. We can be passionate about a lot of things that may not benefit our career, but I don't see those as true passions. I used to be passionate about singing and dancing and music, and I still love going to the theater, but it's just a hobby.

Discovering my true passions that lead to my professional success was a deeper journey and key to finding my destiny. Finding my passion to lead required boldness and tenacity. It is a good thing that I had learned tenacity in college. Tenacity and boldness are cousins. They're family members who enjoy each other's company.

Oh yeah, I forgot to mention, I had never won an Emmy before and had no idea how to win one. More details about that are coming up in the "Defer your need to know how" chapter.

I got the job and the nightmare began. You've heard the phrase, "be careful what you wish for." Well, I was about to live that phrase out.

The team was decades older than me and many had their eyes on retirement, not on working harder to win Emmy awards. People made nasty accusations about me and my character was challenged daily.

A new videographer that had been hired right before I started told me, the rest of the team told him not to talk to me with anything more than yes or no answers, so that I would live quickly like the last executive producer.

Every day my life was difficult, but my boss spoke words of encouragement into me and I'm not sure he realized then that those words were fueling my passion and desire and creating something new in me.

He said, "This is going to be a way different place a year from now and remember, you're running a marathon, not a 50 yard dash.."

Because of the issues I was facing with this team, I was sent to meet with a labor lawyer and human resource experts. I was scared to death. But I was learning on the job that a lot of change and learning was needed, before my dream of leading the team to receiving Emmys was going to come true. You see I never doubted that it would happen. It wasn't IF we'd when Emmys it was WHEN. My passion helped me think that way.

I was brought in to help move the organization in a new direction, but the implications of accidentally saying or doing something that could bring a lawsuit on the station were horrifying. I took one step at a time and I learned a lot, at least enough that protected us from any legal issues.

I was still struggling to create a way to encourage my team to buy into my plans. The reality is, sometimes people just won't buy into your plans, and what they have to do is leave in order to discover their passion somewhere else.

"Skills are cheap. Passion is priceless." Gary Vaynerchuk

I knew I needed to learn a lot more, so I signed up for a one day seminar on "How to Deal with Difficult People." My life was forever changed for the better the day I attended that workshop. It was the first step to creating my professional growth plan that allowed me to discover my passion for leadership. At the end of the day, the facilitator said if you liked what you learned, please check out the resource table at the back of the room.

I bought a John Maxwell book that day.

It was his all-time best seller, *The 21 Irrefutable Laws of Leadership*. It taught me so much, but after I read it, I stopped searching for success and started searching for significance. Things would never be the same for me and I couldn't stop reading. One book after another taught me how to not manage people, but truly lead them and myself.

My, how my life was changed. The staff began to change too, and I was able to hire new members and create my own team.

If I hadn't been struggling with my staff, I never would have attended that seminar. That very difficult time in my life was necessary, I'll even say critical to help me discover my passion. I'm not alone in this thinking. Many great leaders have shared that during their most difficult days, they discovered or uncovered the most impactful things in life.

The number one characteristic I looked for when hiring new members of my team was passion for storytelling. That's something I knew I couldn't teach.

In fact, if you don't have passion for what you do, chances are you're in the wrong job.

If you haven't found your passion yet, here are some tips from Lifehack.com.
1. Is there something you already love doing?
2. What do you spend hours reading about?
3. Brainstorm
4. Ask around and surf for possibilities.
5. Test your idea/but don't quit your job yet.
6. Give it a try/create a side hustle.
7. Research your idea.
8. Practice, practice, practice

Back to my growth plan. I kept reading John's books. They spoke to my soul. I wouldn't just read them. I'd write my version of Cliff Notes and hold staff meetings in order to teach what I had learned to my team.

Little did I know what I was doing was the first step toward unleashing my passion to lead my own professional development company nearly 20 years later. I had developed a young team of reporters, editors and videographers. They looked to me for advice to help them develop their skills. They were hungry and so was I. I had to keep reading so I had something to teach them. I couldn't teach what I didn't know.

Earlier, I shared that research is an important step to find your passion. In the midst of my research, I found I had a passion for learning. It was ignited through reading John's books and I'm grateful that it still burns brightly today, decades later.

I want to take a second to make sure you understand my love of learning isn't just to be able to say that I learned something, it's so I can solve problems. I often call myself a professional problem solver and every day is an opportunity to perfect my problem solving skills. I am a fixer and I can't fix something if I don't know how, so I turn to reading a lot, to find out how to solve my problems.

I've found that finding ways to solve problems leads to success and can be the fastest way to advance your goals. In fact, Harvard Business Review shares having good problem solving skills makes you a desirable candidate for any career.

Back to my team. It took a couple years to get that first regional Mid-Atlantic Emmy nomination with our team and we lost three times before we finally won an Emmy for a documentary we produced. But I am humbled and honored to have led that team to six regional Emmys in Philadelphia before leaving that station. I poured my heart and soul into it for 14 years and really never thought I would leave.

But I had discovered a new passion burning inside of me, to learn all I could to become a PBS General Manager one day. The GM who eventually hired me in Bethlehem spoke that over me. I've thanked him many times, but I'd like to say it here too.

James Baum, I wouldn't be where I am today if you hadn't extended your belief in me. I borrowed your belief, until I could develop my own.

James moved on after a couple years. At that time, I was nowhere near ready to lead a station, but a passionate dream was born. Some choose a leadership path for power and prestige, but I wanted it because I was passionate for people and service. It wasn't about me. It was about me helping others' dreams come true.

Motivational speaker and author **Zig Ziglar said, "You will get all you want in life, if you help enough other people get what they want."** He had a ton of great quotes. I'm going to sprinkle passion quotes throughout the rest of this chapter. I hope you'll find them as motivating as I do.

"I would rather die of passion than of boredom."
Vincent Van Gogh

"People with great passion make the impossible happen." Author Unknown

Passion Killers

Do you really believe you can make the impossible happen? You should. Will it be easy? NO! Will people do everything you ask them to? NO! Will you have your heart broken a million times? Yes! And will you be so hurt by others that you'll want to give up? Yep to that too.

Not having realistic expectations can kill your passion. Knowing that following your passion will most likely be the toughest thing you'll ever do will help you do it. If your expectation is that this road is going to be filled with potholes, then, you won't be devastated or surprised when you get a flat tire.

You've got to choose to look at the positive. You can be bitter or you can be better. I try my best to be better. Anger is the most worthless emotion in my mind. It only hurts you and your passion. It doesn't hurt the person who hurt you.

It's not that I don't get angry, I do, but I try my best to let it go when I go to bed at night. When I wake up the next day I want to focus on solving the problem.

By now, you might be saying, "So what? You found your passion, but I don't know how to find mine?"

I gave you an example of how I found one of my key passions by accident and through problems. You might find yours the same way. I hope I can help you find it a little more quickly and intentionally than I did.

I've shared my passions for leading, learning and problem solving and they're all related and work in tandem. I wouldn't be an effective leader if I couldn't solve problems. I learned how to solve problems, because I had plenty of them and I sought out answers through reading a lot. My passion for people is what sent me down the leadership path to begin with. My passions have focus.

What you're passionate about as a career needs focus too.

Here's another Maxwell quote that means the world to me. **"There are two great days in a person's life, the day you were born and the day you find out why."**

When you find out why you were born, you discover your passion. I found my "why" at that Pennsylvania Public Television station.

Why do you think you were born? Can you define it?

Passion Saves Lives

Greatness to me is the ability to make a positive impact on another person's life. I learned in college that I had a knack for encouraging people. Now that doesn't mean I blow sunshine. You know what I mean when I say sunshine. The person who says something nice, but doesn't really believe it or mean it. I love giving authentic compliments and have tried to take the time to frequently send cards to people. I should have bought stock in Hallmark years ago.

In my 20s, I sang in my church choir. I noticed one of the men had been missing for several weeks. He was married and had a young daughter. I asked the church office if I gave them a card would they mail it to his home address. The secretary agreed to help me. The card was just a little "thinking of you" card. I don't remember exactly what it said, but several months later he came up to me in church, hugged me, and said that card saved his life.

He told me that he had been planning to commit suicide and the day he had determined to do so, my card arrived. He felt like if an acquaintance had cared about him, he needed to care about himself and his family, and that life was worth living.

You never know how powerful one act of kindness can be or who it can save. In this case, God used my passion for people, to literally save a man's life. I think that makes me great. I know if you just give it some thought you will see things that will make you great too. Those things will lead you to discover your unique passion.

"Nothing is as important as passion. No matter what you want to do with your life, be passionate." Jon Bon Jovi

"The most successful people follow passion, not paychecks." Jen Welter NFL's first female coach

Discovering your passion often begins by realizing what it's not. It's not a hobby or simply what you're good at doing. Those are stepping stones to finding your passion. I loved arts and crafts as a kid but that wasn't what I was passionate about.

Condolezza Rice served as the 66th United States Secretary of State, under George W. Bush. She was the first female African American to hold that position. She said, "Whatever you choose to do, you have one other obligation, and that is to yourself. Do it with passion. If you've not yet found your passion, keep searching. You never know when it will find you."

It's funny how many people describe that their passion found them and not the other way around. What makes your heart sing? What can you do all day and feel like only minutes have passed? Pursuing your passion makes you feel fulfilled. Please don't miss this point. I can completely enjoy spending an entire Saturday watching Hallmark movies too. It's enjoyable and relaxing, but that's not fulfilling to me. Do you see the difference?

If you're still stumped, ask the people who matter most to you what they see as your greatest talents. Passion usually is right around the corner from there.

Here's another tip to finding your passion. What recurring thoughts do you have? What do you dream about? Those are passion clues my friends, don't overlook them. Seize them and they will seize you back in the most fulfilling way.

"Always remember you have within you the strength, the patience and the passion to reach for the stars to change the world." Harriet Tubman

Memory Making Moments

Do you feel like you've discovered your passion or are you still looking for it? Sometimes exercises help clarify things.

Write down the most defining moment in your life. Was it a positive or a negative? How did it make you feel? Have you had other similar moments? If so, you're getting closer to defining your passion.

Do you have a nagging feeling that you just can't get rid of? Does it keep coming back every few months or at the beginning of every new year? That feeling is your passion begging you to let it out.

It's not too late and you're never too old. As long as you still have breath, there's time to walk into your great destiny. But the key is to follow the advice of Walt Disney and stop putting it off until tomorrow.

Before we move on to our next D, let's recap what we've learned. Remember when I told you I praised God after not getting the job I really wanted? Showing gratitude during your darkest times reveals powerful things in your life and it can lead you to your passion.

The next thing you need to discern is the difference between your passion and your hobbies. It will definitely take some time but you can do it.

Discovering your passion definitely takes time, thought, conversation with friends and family, and a look back at recurring themes in your life.

Another way I want to sum up this chapter is to give you a mental picture of the power of your passion. When tapped correctly and effectively, it will become one of the most powerful forces of nature that you can witness.

To help imagine that power, I want you to think of a waterfall. Whether it's Niagara Falls or one near you, what they all have in common is the immense power they create. They literally change the landscape. Elements as tough as granite are no match for a waterfall.

When you harness your passion, it will have the same power. I think you'll be amazed at the satisfaction it will give you.

"People with great passion make the impossible happen." Author Unknown

Unleashing your passion helps you get there.

CHAPTER 3
DEMOLISH NEGATIVE THINKING

"Believing in negative thoughts is the single greatest obstruction to success." Charles F. Glassman

After reading that quote how do you feel about your negative thinking? Does it make you want to stop thinking that way? I hope so. The nadering nabobs of negativity are dream killers. You know what I'm talking about. It's our own stinkin thinkin that often keeps us from walking into our great destiny.

What was the last nice thing you thought about yourself? If you can't think of one, here's an easier question. What was the last negative thought you had about yourself? That shouldn't be an easier question.

You can train yourself to think more positively and your life will be better and not just emotionally. Research shows you'll be better physically too.

According to the Mayo Clinic, here are the health benefits of positive thinking.

1. Increased life span
2. Lower rates of depression
3. Lower levels of distress
4. Greater resistance to the common cold
5. Better psychological and physical well-being
6. Better cardiovascular health and reduced risk of death from cardiovascular disease
7. Better coping skills during hardships and times of stress.

Have I convinced you yet, that it's worth the effort to change your thinking?

It's not going to happen over night and it's not easy to get rid of some of the most common negative thoughts like... "I'm too old to chase my dreams." "I don't have the talent or money to chase my dreams." "I never should have tried."

" I'm destined to fail."

Actually, you are. We ALL fail.

Thomas Edison said, "Many of life's failures are people who did not realize how close they were to success when they gave up."

It took Edison 10,000 tries to invent the light bulb. One day, a reporter asked him how it felt to fail that many times. Edison said, "I didn't fail 10,000 times. The light bulb was an invention with 10,000 steps."

Now that's how you demolish negative thinking!

Your life is too important to waste time with negativity. Sometimes it's your own thoughts, but you want to get away from negative people too. With friends like those, who needs enemies?

It's rarely easy to get away from negative people in your life, but Forbes Magazine has these five tips to stop giving negative people too much power in your life.

1. Guard Your Time
Here's the deal, negative people can suck the life out of you. You know I'm telling the truth. They sap the energy out of you, which isn't helping you find your destiny.

2. Choose Your Attitude
Don't allow the negative people in your life to dictate the way you feel about things. You have the power to choose

how you feel. Make a declaration that you're going to have a great day in spite of them and your circumstances.

3. Refocus Your Thoughts
Here's a question for you. How do your thoughts change when you're around negative people? Let's be honest, they don't make you feel good. Make a decision that you're not going to waste your time and energy thinking like them.

4. Choose Productivity
Those negative people in our lives often bring out the worst in us. You may be angry about how they make you feel, but is that helping your situation? Control your emotions. Take them captive so you can make decisions that allow you to move forward and enjoy your life.

5. Find Positive People
This one's my favorite, because I'm an extravert who loves making new friends. However, introverts can do it too. It's a choice and you have the power to choose who you spend time with usually. Perhaps you have negative family members. Yes, you may have to live in the same house as them, but you can seek out positive people to spend your free time with.

Set the expectation that this is hard work, but it's worth the effort. You'll probably fail at it too and that's ok. Failure is inevitable, but it's not the end, if you keep trying. It's actually the first step toward success.

One of my favorite John Maxwell books, I confess to having a lot of favorites, is FAILING FORWARD. I think it was 2002 when I read it the first time. I loved it.

It was filled with stories of people failing many times before succeeding, yet they weren't negative people. They included people like Truett Cathy, founder of Chick-fil-A.

Cathy struggled a lot before creating his fast food giant. He served in the army, then created the Dwarf Grill. Shortly after opening the restaurant, his brother, who was also his business partner, died in a plane crash with his other brother.

That's a crushing life event, but it got worse. He then discovered he had an illness. He had polyps in his colon. He had two surgeries and while spending months recovering, he discovered his mega-million dollar idea to create a chain of restaurants based around a fried, seasoned chicken breast and the rest, as they say, is history. It makes my mouth water just thinking about that franchise.

Truett Cathy could have just felt sorry for himself, because of all of his challenges and fallen into a habit of negativity, but he didn't. He channeled his disappointment into positive forward movement.

I loved FAILING FORWARD, but I hated the title so when I did a workshop for my staff about the book, I renamed it, "Searching for Success".

Maxwell says failing is a part of life and a necessary step toward success. It's unavoidable, but I did everything I could not to have that dirty "F" word in my life. It took me at least another decade to warm up to that concept.

Remember, failing isn't final unless you let it become final. Look at a lack of immediate success as just learning how not to do something.

Your reaction to failure is critically important. You must stay positive, no matter how difficult or ugly the situation becomes. Look for the lessons in every failed attempt. Ask yourself what you learned. It's hard, but it is vital.

One of the defining moments of my life happened in college. I always wanted to be a television broadcaster, but my single mom during the 1970s told me women should be school teachers or nurses. She happened to be a nurse. Both are great professions that help a lot of people, but they weren't what I dreamed about.

My mom loved me, but she wanted to protect me from television, because she saw it as a field she thought might be too difficult. She wanted me to have a way to provide for myself. My dad walked out on her and three little girls when I was just 18 months old and he declared bankruptcy.

Thank heavens my mom was a registered nurse and had great hard working, God loving parents who allowed us to move in with them.

Note to self, moms always know best. They can see talents in you that you may not see for yourself. She knew I had teaching in my blood and I ended up doing some adjunct broadcast teaching in a few colleges decades later and I loved teaching my teams.

While my mom saw that I had potential to be a good teacher, she missed that my greatest passion at the time was to pursue a career in broadcasting. Later in life, those two talents merged into my evolved passion.

I think I learned from my mom's failed marriage, that education was critical to providing a better future for yourself. That's an interesting thing about failing, you can learn from other people's failures too.

Now let's get back to my journey with the "Dirty F-Word."

My high school guidance counselor, Pam Swinderman, connected the dots of my life and gave me the courage to pursue a degree in Broadcast Journalism. She saw my potential and that I had always been a writer and that I had participated in school plays. She knew I had developed pretty good public speaking skills and thought I could combine two of my talents into a successful career.

I told you earlier it took me five tries to pass my "Entrance to Journalism" exam my freshman year of college. Meanwhile, I was writing front page stories for our daily school newspaper, but I couldn't pass that silly test.

I had myself so sick over the whole thing that when I finally passed, I was convinced the school still wouldn't let me in. After I passed the test, I was called before the journalism review board. I was terrified. I imagined every bad outcome in my head. I thought they would never allow someone as stupid as me to be admitted into the program. I had fallen into a negative pit for a while, but I didn't stay there.

> **"Dwelling on the negative simply contributes to its power."**
>
> *Shirley MacLaine*

Much to my surprise, the professors not only let me into the program, they also discontinued the test. I was young and a little selfish and didn't see how powerful my failed attempts would be toward helping others. No one else would have to be so freaked out about passing an exam that they would cause themselves to fail.

They told me I had proven I had the most important thing that I needed to be successful in journalism and that was tenacity. I had to fail to win so I would learn what Winston Churchill said.

"Never, ever, ever give up." Winston Churchill

That early failure was pivotal in finding my destiny. I know I wouldn't be where I am today, if I hadn't failed that college test. In hindsight, I'm grateful, but it's taken me a long time to be able to see that to change my thinking from believing I was a failure to recognizing that the test was a setup to my success.

All of the SEVEN D's to your Destiny work together, laying stepping stones guiding you to your future. My desire and my passion helped me demolish my negative thinking.

Let me rephrase that, I still have to be careful not to trash talk myself, but my passion to help others actually helps me too. When I realized that others needed me to walk into my destiny, it seemed more important for me to get there than if I was just doing it for myself. That lesson was cemented in the fiber of my being from that day on.

I have to confess, I was more than a little angry that no one else would have to suffer like I did. But as I've aged, I couldn't help but ask myself how many people are in journalism, because of me and my failure. Nearly 20 year later I was teaching a high school broadcast class and one of my students shared that her aunt went to my school and was my age. She had failed that entrance to journalism test too and was about to change her major, when she learned the test was no longer necessary to be in the program. WOW! My failure has made a positive impact on others. She wasn't planning on taking it again, she was going to change her major. But thanks to my failure, she didn't have to look for a new career. She went on to be a successful ABC anchor in Philadelphia. That early failure of mine actually launched me, and others, toward success.

"Negative words are powerful boomerangs so be careful what you say about people and yourself."
Mary J Blige

Many, many times I've had to demolish my own negative thinking. You will too. But fear not, you can do it! The more you do it, the better you get at it.

However, this is not a one-time thing. You will need to hone this talent to do it several times, whenever needed. It seems I always have to do it again. It never really goes away completely. I'm way better at recognizing it before it gets out of control and I do my best to squash it like a bug. One strategy that always helps me is to remind myself that I was created for GREATNESS and so were YOU!

Four Steps to Undo Negative Thoughts

What negative thoughts do you need to demolish? Here are four steps to help you find out and set them for demolition.

First, practice saying five nice things about yourself each day. I realize it sounds corny, but do it anyway.

I turn to the Bible for this a lot. "You were fearfully and wonderfully made," Psalm 149:14 is one of my favorites. So is Jeremiah 29:11, "For I know the plans I have for you, declares the Lord. Plans to prosper you and not to harm you, plans to give you hope and a future."

Wherever you find your spiritual inspiration, you will find ideas to help you build a better self image.

Here are a couple more strategies. First, reframe your thinking. One way to do that is to surround yourself with positive quotes that will lead you to more positive thoughts. I always get inspired when I read something that naturally lifts me up.

Here's another technique. Exercise always works for me. When I need to clear my head, I take a walk. How do you supercharge your walk? Find a beautiful place to do it and listen to a podcast that will shift your thinking.

Next, try this little exercise that won't require sweat, and can absolutely help you defeat the mind monsters inside of you. It made a huge difference for me.

Get a rubber band and wear it on your wrist like a bracelet for a month. It's not a fashion statement. It's a tool.

Every time you think a negative thought, flick the rubber band on your wrist. Try not to leave too big of a welt. Just do it hard enough to sting a little. Over time, you'll condition yourself not to think negatively.

Here's the third step. I look back on my life and see how many things I've overcome. It's easy for us to forget how many challenges we have overcome.

For me and my faith, I figure if God brought me through those trials, he'll get me through my current situation, whatever it may be. God won't quit on you. He's going to finish what he started in you and through you. Deuteronomy 31:8 states, "I will never leave you nor forsake you." That statement gives me the courage to keep trying.

All of us have great examples of things we have overcome. Looking at how far you've come and recognizing your own progress really helps.

Finally, I try to avoid saying negative absolutes about myself like, 'you'll NEVER be able to do that' or 'you must be the dumbest person on Earth'. I still slip up sometimes, but usually I can capture those thoughts and squash them pretty quickly these days. With practice, you will too.

"My model for business is The Beatles: They were four guys that kept each others' negative tendencies in check; they balanced each other. And the total was greater than the sum of the parts." Steve Jobs

I'm blessed to have the opportunity to attend Elevation Church in Charlotte, North Carolina. I love learning from Pastor Steven Furtick. I've read all of his books.

A recent sermon was titled, "Knock Knock." It's absolutely worth looking up on YouTube.

He said, "It's easier for you to believe you're worthless, than you're created for greatness."

That type of negative thinking has to go! We've got to kick it to the curb, once and for all.

I'll say it again, everything is temporary, short of death. You can overcome anything if you're tenacious enough to keep trying and keep learning from your mistakes.

So let's recap. Here's a reminder why it's worth the effort to demolish negative thinking. Your health depends on it. You'll live longer if you do. You'll reduce your risk for depression and you'll be able to handle stress better.

It's hard enough to control your own negative thoughts, but we need to stop giving negative people too much power in our lives too. Remember to guard your time. Nobody can tell you to have a bad attitude. You are the master of your attitude, so choose to think about the positive.

Make the choice to be productive. Accomplish things every day, even if it means just starting with the simple task of making your bed. And, by all means, hang out with people who lift you up as opposed to those who walk around life with a dark cloud hanging over their heads.

Once you reduce the external negativity from the people around you, you can focus on robbing the power from your own negative thoughts. Start by seeing yourself in a positive light. Begin each day by saying five nice things about yourself. Take captive every negative thought. Imagine yourself in the positivity rodeo and you've got to lasso every single negative thought.

Make sure to put some exercise in your life, thirty minutes a day helps your brain produce more endorphins that will make you feel good.

And finally, put a rubber band on your wrist and flick yourself every time those mind monsters try to tell you that you can't do it. Soon, you'll condition yourself to think more positively.

You can demolish your negative thinking with training. Start training today. I promise you it's worth the effort and necessary, if you're serious about walking into your great destiny.

CHAPTER 4
DEFER YOUR NEED TO KNOW HOW

"Life is about not knowing, having to change, taking the moment and making the best of it, without knowing what's going to happen next." Gilda Radner

Think about this for a minute. Does it sound terrifying to you? As a planner I confess, it's a little scary, but oh so rewarding. What if you wanted to learn how to golf, but refused to step on the course until you had the swing of Jack Nicklaus or if you wanted to learn how to swim, but wouldn't jump into a pool, because you hadn't won an Olympic medal like Michael Phelps?

Both of those examples probably seem a little silly, but so is waiting for the perfect moment to get started. Waiting until you know everything to finally do something is one of the greatest hurdles to finding your destiny. You can make yourself wait to be an expert and may wait so long that your destiny passes you by.

You are not alone in your fears. Many of us want to know every step to take before we start any journey, but all we really need to do is take the first step. Then, keep putting one foot in front of the other. Experiment, practice and get better. Then, repeat.

Here's a warning, chances are that the first step will come with challenges. It's unlikely that you'll figure it all out perfectly in the beginning. You'll need some encouragement to keep you moving forward. This is where mastering the previous chapter on how to defeat disappointment really comes in handy. If you set the right expectations, it's often easier to handle disappointments.

Steven Furtick's "Knock Knock" sermon that I told you about earlier should help. "Faith is getting dressed, even when you don't know where you're going. When opportunity comes to the door, opposition comes with it," he told us. It's important that you realize that it is a key part of the journey.

One of the first steps to my destiny came from a challenging staff. I didn't know how to lead a team of people at my first PBS station back in Pennsylvania. I made tons of mistakes and they weren't cutting me any slack. However, if it weren't for those challenges, I never would have attended the "How to Deal with Difficult People" seminar. If I hadn't attended that seminar, I wouldn't have discovered John Maxwell's books and if I hadn't read his books and fallen in love with his teachings, my husband would never have given me the best gift ever.

My husband gave me a one year membership to John's Maximum Impact Club and the monthly CD's lead me to a man named Paul Martinelli, the creator of the John Maxwell Team of certified trainers, speakers and coaches.

Paul invited me to join his team and I continue to invest in myself through its mentorship program, which helps me to continue to grow and share what I learn with others. The mentorship program keeps my mind in the right place so I can keep moving forward.

I first heard the phrase, "suspend your need to know how," from Paul. He used to say, "Jump, and build your wings on the way down." I wasn't a fan of the saying in the beginning, but it grew on me and in me. I was afraid the advice wasn't responsible, but I just didn't get it at first.

"Sometimes surrender means giving up trying to understand and becoming comfortable with not knowing." Eckhart Tolle

At that time in my life, I still didn't fully understand what deferring your "need to know how" meant. Being in the mentorship program and building a relationship with a team of people through weekly calls taught me how to defer my need to know how. I was part of a community of people sharing how they were actually doing it every day. Being a part of this community gave me the confidence to try and the awareness I needed to better understand the concept.

You will need to find a community to foster your success too. There are lots of online options these days. All you have to do is search online for groups for achievers or entrepreneurs or whatever you're trying to figure out how to do that you've never done before.

My favorite place to connect with like minded people is through Facebook. I mentioned earlier that I have my certification as a John Maxwell Trainer, Speaker and Coach and I get so much out of that community. I struggle with digital marketing so I joined the Digital Marketing Mentorship group created by my friend Dave Gambrill, another friend I made through JMT.

I've also created one with you in mind to go along with this book. If you search Facebook for "The 7D's to Your Destiny," you'll find a ton of positivity and people in all professions encouraging one another to take risks and defer their need to know how.

So how do we become comfortable with not knowing how to make our dreams our reality from the beginning? And what does it take to truly get what it means to defer your need to know how? First, you've just got to get comfortable with being uncomfortable.

For me, the answers came in trying new things, things I had never done before and accomplishing them. Winning my first regional Emmy in Philadelphia was a pivotal moment back in 2002. I had been a television reporter/producer for 12 years before it happened. I'd been nominated twice and that third nomination turned into my first beautiful gold statue.

It's not an exact science, nothing in life is. I've lost more Emmys than I've won, but I'm honored to share that I've led teams to earn ten Emmys.

Here's my recipe for accomplishing something new. You may need to tweak it for yourself but it's worth a try.

Begin by focusing on growing yourself. This journey is going to create a better version of yourself and you have to get ready for it. Next, concentrate on learning. Read a book, take a class, sign up for a webinar. Do anything to expand your current knowledge, specifically about what you're passionate about and what you don't know how to do. Now, you're ready for the final steps, trust me, they are the hardest. Add a lot of patience, because learning anything new takes time. The other ingredient that you will need in bulk is perseverance. It's definitely a long and winding road, with plenty of speed bumps, detours and potholes. Don't give up and persevere! It's been a winning recipe for me.

Now I realize that looks too easy to be successful, but the real trick is consistency. I've been doing those things for more than three decades.

When you don't know how to start a business, write a book or win an Emmy, take one step and one of two things will happen. Either that first step will lead you to your next step or you'll figure out that wasn't the right first step and you'll know that you need to go in a different direction. Either way, you will be one step closer to your dream. Again, do not let failing in the first step stop you. That misstep is helping you find the right step!

When toddlers are learning to walk, they fall down a lot, but that doesn't keep them from learning how to walk. They get up and take another step and fall down again, and again, and again until they figure it out.

That's all we're doing too, but for some strange reason, it seems so much harder as adults. It seems our toddler selves had it right all along. They knew how to defer their need to know how and just started trying and kept at it.

My life has been filled with doing things successfully that I had never done before. I didn't know how to do it when I took the first step. I didn't get it right the first time, or the tenth time in many cases. But with personal growth, time and patience, trial and error, persistence and prayer, I figured a lot of things out.

As a kid, I asked "why" a lot. It drove my mom crazy. I was inquisitive and creative, some, like my sisters, would say to a fault.

I remember being bored one day in elementary school and I decided to make my own doll from a sock, scraps of fabric and yarn. My mom asked me, "How do you know how to make a doll?" And I said, "I don't." But I was doing it. I had no idea back then that it was a set up to me finding and fulfilling my destiny.

Here's a story about another woman who had never made a doll before.

Do you know the name Ruth Handler? I suspect not. One day, while watching her daughter Barbara play grown up with some paper dolls, she got the idea to invent the Barbie Doll. She had never made a doll before, but that didn't stop her. That doll became the best selling doll of all time and put Ruth's husband's company on the map, a little company called Mattel.

I've always loved to write. In elementary school, I wrote plays on carbon paper. If you're under 50, chances are that the idea of carbon paper is a foreign term to you. As I recall, there were five white pieces of paper in between pieces of carbon paper, which when written on, would copy what was written on all the pages.

I hand wrote the story on the front sheet and it made five copies. Nobody had a personal printer back then. Because of the limitations of carbon paper to five sheets at a time, there could never be more than five characters in my plays so that I could give everyone their own script.

I didn't know HOW to write a play. I just decided to tell a story that was in my mind. I'd turn to the Encyclopedia Britannica. (That's what people did before Google) I'd look up facts about a subject and weave them in and out with my imagination.

Now, my first few plays would never have won an award. But the more I wrote, the better the stories became. I decided to enter an essay contest in the third grade. Again, my mom worried if I could do it, because I'd never done it before. At that age, I had no doubt in myself so I entered the contest with no hesitation. And guess what? I won! I entered another essay contest in the fifth grade and I won that one too.

Fast forward to my sophomore year of high school. I wanted to enter a pageant. I raced home, excited to tell my mom. Her response was, "But what will you do for your talent?"

She wasn't trying to be mean. She was right, I hadn't shown any signs of possible pageant talent before.

I told her that I was going to sing. I had always sung in chorus, but I had never sung a solo before, so I set out to learn how. My high school chorus teacher stayed after school and helped me. Guess what? I won that pageant!

Now, before you get jaded and say I'm just one of those people where everything works out for them, let me tell you that I am very, very familiar with failure. I entered many pageants that I didn't win. I applied for many jobs that I didn't get. And don't get me started on how many awards I have entered that I didn't win.

My secret is that I have learned how to not let failure or not knowing how to do something stop me from trying again. That's the secret I'm sharing with you in this book.

I think those early years of succeeding at achieving certain goals built a great foundation to do bigger things.

No success rarely, if ever, came on the first time. But with research, a thirst for learning, strategy and a tremendous amount of effort, I made it work. When I didn't hit the mark, I carefully reevaluated and pivoted to a new direction.

I see dreams like rings on a bullseye. I take aim, throw the dart, but rarely do I hit the bullseye on the first throw. I felt if I could hit any of the rings on the target, I was moving in the right direction. If I was getting closer to the goal, I should just try again and again until I made it happen.

I love dreaming about bigger things, but dreaming is just the start. I love achieving them even more. I've got to admit, being driven is both a blessing and a curse.

With all the heartbreaking failures, I never lost that internal crazy belief that somehow, some way I can make this happen, whatever "this" is.

Actually, you are reading proof of that tenacity right now. This is my first book and I literally had to defer the need to know how to do it. Since you're reading it now, that means I did it and I already have a title for my second book. But I'm keeping it a secret for now.

Not being able to let go of an idea is another sign that you're walking toward your destiny. It's not just a passing whim.

I'm willing to bet that you probably have that internal feeling too, but perhaps you've stopped listening to it. I'm begging you to stop stifling your inner voice that is telling you there is something more out there for you.

Let me rephrase that. If you're anything like me, and I believe you are, you probably hear two voices.

One voice tells you that you can do this, and the other tells you that you can't.

When I was younger, I don't ever remember thinking that I couldn't do something. That internal doubt developed the older I became due to things not happening as quickly as I would have liked.

Dreams deferred aren't dead, they are simply just not meant for right now. However, the older we get, the more difficult it becomes to visualize our dreams and the more difficult it is to take a step toward them, especially if we've failed trying before.

This is where the bullseye I described earlier comes in. You need to visualize yourself succeeding. See yourself hitting that bullseye, one step at a time.

"Not knowing when the dawn will come I open every door." Emily Dickinson

Author Emily Dickinson surely knew what she was writing with that last quotation. Opening every door is another important step. It will help you avoid having regrets in your life too, because you'll know you never missed an opportunity.

Another important step you can take is visualization. I visualized myself on stage accepting an Emmy years before I was ever nominated for one. That belief was not overconfidence, it was healthy audacity.

I want you to have that healthy audacity to convince your biggest critic, yourself, that you can do it! If audacity is a new concept for you, I want to help you master it. It means a willingness to take bold risks. I realize most people aren't risk takers.   They want to play it safe...not rock the boat and I don't know anyone who likes to be told no. I certainly don't. When you've been told no 10 times and you still won't quit, that's the type of healthy audacity I'm talking about.

Here are a couple examples from my life. As the head of a PBS station, I do a lot of fundraising. I'll ask anyone for money to help our mission of educating, inspiring and entertaining our region.   I had a healthcare organization give us $125,000 one year and I was asking them to give the same amount the following year. They seemed to like what we had created, but communications went radio silent for several months. I sent an email every week and left a voicemail every other week. Four months had passed and still no word from my contact.   It was Good Friday and I had the day off. Something inside me said try one last time. I sent an email that went something like this.

Dear Emily,

I'm so very sorry to keep reaching out. I know how busy you are so I thought I'd try one last time to see if you'd like to renew our partnership for another year. If I don't hear from you, I'll take that as confirmation that you don't want to work with us to serve our region in this way and that you're not interested. It has been my great pleasure to collaborate to empower our region to take control of their health. I hope you and your family enjoy a wonderful Easter.

Warmest Regards,

Amy

She responded to my email in one hour, and agreed to renew her sponsorship for another year. This huge contract would have simply disappeared, if I didn't have healthy audacity.

Here's another example. When I had the idea to create my high school career pathways and leadership program, The 3D Project: Dreamers-Doers-Destiny, I went to over a dozen businesses asking for financial support. Every one of them said it sounded like a good idea, but expressed concern that I had never created anything like this before. They each told me NO, but that didn't stop me.

The passion I had burning inside me to help this generation of at risk-youth wouldn't let me take no for an answer. I kept looking for other funding streams. I wrote a federal grant and received $100,000 a year for three years. Over 500 teens have now been empowered with tools to choose a better life for themselves through this program.

Oh yeah, I forgot to mention, I had never written a federal grant before. I didn't know how, but I deferred my need to know how and I just let my passion take over and it worked.

As we get older, we often become too practical, and when we don't know how to do something, we stop trying.

Some days, those horrible thoughts of failing can get the best of you and me. But other days I believe GOD smacks me upside the head and whispers, "Amy, it's time to dream again. Get started NOW."

And then I say the worst thing I could ever say, and I'm a slow learner, because I still say it too often.

"BUT I DON'T KNOW HOW."

What a lousy statement. I have a lifetime of experiences, and I bet you do too, that prove that your inner voice is a no good filthy liar. I have spent my entire career successfully doing things I didn't know how to do. I didn't realize that until right before my 50th birthday. I want to help you figure it out a lot quicker than I did, because it is such a powerful awareness. While I didn't realize that's what I was doing, I just kept doing things I'd never done before over and over and over again until I built the confidence to try new things.

This book has been my dream for a long time and I want you to know how good it feels to prove to that inner doubting voice that I did it. You are reading how I have proved that negative inner voice wrong. If I can do it, so can you!

I liked to read growing up, but I didn't love it and it wasn't until I graduated college and had nine years of experience as a commercial television anchor and reporter, that I fell in love with reading. Actually, it wasn't the reading that I loved so much, it was the learning that came from reading that became my addiction. It was the absolute best kind of addiction.

Earlier, I told you how honored I've been to lead my teams in Pennsylvania and North Carolina to ten regional Emmys. We beat network affiliates with huge budgets and hundreds of employees with our tiny teams and puny budgets.

But I created a lot of bad television before I figured out how to make it better and then we worked hard to just keep getting better. Continuous improvement is part of the culture of every organization I lead.

Commitment to personal and professional growth leads to accomplishing new things we've never done before, every day. Once you remove the fear of trying something new, everything gets easier and you get momentum on your side.

Stick with me for a moment. I'm going to take you somewhere important I promise. I believe our destiny constantly evolves and our need to defer how to do things will grow more important over time. What we're doing now prepares us for what's next. Our purpose in our 20s, most likely isn't our purpose in our 40s and 50s. This can be problematic for we type "A" personalities, but with time we can learn to be like Disney's Mrs. Incredible, flexible.

When I learn something in a book, I'm compelled to share it with others and put it into practice even though I most likely have never done that particular thing before.

As a growth junkie, that means I'm always trying to grow myself and do things I've never done before, I struggle when team members don't want to tackle new things.

It's a concept completely foreign to me. People who do not see the value of growing, baffle me.

Reading helped me develop a growth mindset, which led to me learning how to defer my need to know how. It often comes in steps. It taught me not to seek success, but to strive for significance. Once you've tasted that, you'll never want to be just successful again.

"I actually like not knowing. I trust every lead." Dan Scanlan

Unfortunately, too many people just want to survive. I believe it's because they have no clue how extraordinary they will feel when they start to THRIVE.

Thriving requires intense effort and the ability to look at yourself and admit that you have more to give and more to learn and so much more to gain if you do both. It takes us back to the title of this chapter. You need to defer the need to know how.

Remember, faith is getting dressed even when you don't know where you're going. Take the time to find a community that will help you online. Look back over your life at all the things you accomplished not knowing how. It started when you learned to walk and talk. You had no clue how to do those things, but somehow you did them.

I know if you try, you can come up with a lot of other things that will build your confidence to continue to try new things. I can't imagine my life without Barbie dolls. They helped me create dreams through play as a child. I'm so glad Ruth Handler invented the Barbie doll even though she had never done anything like that before. Playing with that doll launched me into a life of possibilities.

Don't forget that most people hear two voices in their head. Fear not, you're perfectly normal. However, you've got to only listen to the voice that leads you toward a future with you finding your great destiny.

Just because you couldn't make something work a dozen times doesn't mean it's not meant to be. Dreams deferred aren't dead. It's just not the right time for them yet.

Once you bond with the concept and taste the wins of accomplishing things you've never done before, I predict you'll be hooked.

It doesn't make it any less scary, but the reward of feeling significant is ohhhhh so satisfying. Come on, and get started now. If I can do it, I know you can too. Be brave and defer your need to know how.

CHAPTER 5
DEVELOP DISCIPLINE

"Discipline is the bridge between goals and accomplishment." – Jim Rohn

Let the discipline training begin.

The Nike mission statement is, "Bring inspiration and innovation to every athlete in the world." Nike sees everyone as an athlete. Do you see yourself that way? Athletes know a lot about discipline. They train their bodies, not just when they feel like it, but every day. Can you say that about yourself? If you don't already see yourself as an athlete, can you start to see yourself that way now?

Let's start by agreeing to be in training to find your destiny.

If you see yourself in training to find your destiny, you can use that as a visual image to remind you that you don't just wake up one morning and find that your dreams and goals just magically came true. Finding your destiny requires hard work and discipline to get there and I know you can do it.

At my age I'm not going to win an Olympic Medal in track and field, but I do my best to stay in shape. Jazzercize, dance aerobics, is my sport of choice. Most weeks, I go five times a week for an hour. It helps me de-stress and I physically and mentally feel better afterwards. I've been doing it for three years. It's officially a habit and I miss it when I don't go.

Good habits require discipline. But what keeps us on track when we don't see results for weeks, months or sometimes years? That's where chapter one comes in again and we allow our DESIRE to push us through the difficult days. I've shared that all of these seven D's work in conjunction with each other and desire helps us develop discipline to make our dreams and our destiny our reality.

"Success is a matter of understanding and religiously practicing specific simple habits that always lead to success." – Robert J. Ringer

Simple habits like being on time. When I was in high school I was in our competitive marching band. It seemed like every Saturday morning in the fall, we had to meet at the school before dawn to jump on the bus and head to some far away city to compete. Our band director Mr. Larry Kelly always said, "to be early is to be on time. To be on time is to be late and to be late is to be left." I never wanted to be left behind so I quickly created the discipline of planning my mornings. The night before, after performing at the football game, I'd clean my shoes. Pack my brown bag lunch and set the alarm. A little pre-planning allowed me to always be a little bit early. Boy, did that early discipline training serve me well over my life.

I've worked with my office manager, Linda Kempf, at three different companies. Somewhere around age 45, she started working with a trainer and lost a lot of weight and looked better than I'd ever seen her. I met her when we both were in our 20s.

Her confidence grew during that time too. She became very disciplined, eating right and exercising. Discipline is like a muscle. It needs training and stretching.

Here's the exciting part, once you grow your discipline muscle, there's no stopping what you can accomplish both personally and professionally.

When Linda began to get in shape, she set a goal for herself, to run a half marathon. After Linda accomplished that, she set a new goal. She wanted to run a full marathon, all 26.2 miles.

I thought she was crazy, but as I watched her train, I saw her take more risks on the job too. She was no longer afraid to tackle bigger projects that she had never done before. She said goodbye to the fear of not being enough and tasted the sweet success that her newly developed discipline muscle that she trained so hard delivered and it brought her professional success too.

In the past, she merely saw herself as a support person who would do anything she was asked. Now she sees herself as a leader and she makes a major positive impact at PBS Charlotte. I'd be lost without her.

"Winners embrace hard work. They love the discipline of it, the trade-off they're making to win. Losers, on the other hand, see it as a punishment. And that's the difference." – Lou Holtz

As my mentor John Maxwell says, "Everything worthwhile is an uphill habit." The opposite is also true. There are downhill habits like smoking, not exercising and taking the easy way out that get you nowhere and can destroy you.

But how do you commit to those uphill habits? I shared this earlier, but it's worth restating. Research shows it takes 21 days to create a habit, both good and bad. After the first 21 days, it gets easier to keep going. That ease comes as a by-product of discipline.

The hardest person you will EVER have to lead is yourself.

You might be thinking that as a leader, I must love discipline? NOPE, but I have learned to bond with it.

Discipline isn't just used for making our bodies strong. We need it to make our minds strong too. What discipline habits can you adopt to make your own mind strong? Reading is one of my favorites. I can hear what you're thinking "I don't have time to do anymore reading."

I'm just like you. I have a busy life with work and family. But how will you grow your mind without feeding it new thoughts and new ideas? Those thoughts and ideas will give you steps to take to make those dreams you've always had realities.

For every excuse, there's a solution. Audio books are an option, but personally I love touching the pages, dog-earring those that speak to me and highlighting impactful thoughts so I can share those thoughts with others in the future. Podcasts are the hottest thing these days. We can learn while sitting in traffic, which makes congestion on the highways far less frustrating.

I love the discipline of planning. I'm a planner. It often drives my family crazy, especially on vacation. Let me break that down a little more. Those of you with teenagers, or as I've said on more than one occasion, mean-agers, may be able to relate to this story.

I can be a little tough to be around on travel days. I have a set schedule that I see as discipline and I back time it for maximum efficiency.

I know my son and husband tend to run a bit late so I always tell them our departure time is 15 minutes earlier than it needs to be in hopes of getting out on my schedule. Don't let them in on my secret. For now, it's just between us.

Over time, my husband has gotten better at prepping for travel days and I've been around him long enough that I've mellowed... a tad.

A recent morning was one of those travel days worthy of sharing.

To celebrate my son's high school graduation, we traveled to San Diego for our family vacation. As anyone with a teenager knows, somehow, he knows everything. We bickered getting out of the house at 5:45 a.m.

It's never the way I imagine these vacations. We were 15 minutes later than we should have been to get to the airport...and that's on top of my 15 minute planned late departure!

We had an issue checking our bags and had to wait in the "special customer " service line, which is always slower.

My son had to have Chick-fil-A for breakfast, which is ALWAYS the longest food line at the airport, and anywhere, I think. Once we had our breakfast, we got to the gate with literally two minutes to spare before boarding. I had never cut it that close before.

My son said, "I told you we'd be fine." He still relies on luck, but I believe luck often comes to the person who had the most discipline to prepare. Bad luck has a way of catching up to the unprepared sooner or later. As Louis Pasteur said, "Fortune favors the prepared mind."

I managed to keep my mouth shut, which doesn't happen very often, because I'm always trying to teach my son a better way. I want to teach him that more discipline in his life will help him make his dreams come true. But, as it is with most of us at that age, he doesn't want to hear it. Does any recent high school graduate really want to hear this?

Some things people have to learn on their own. I think that's the toughest part of being a parent. As someone with a heart and drive to add value to others, I always want to teach. However, people don't always want to learn and that's frustrating for me, especially where my one and only son is involved.

I believe so deeply in his potential, but he has to choose how he'll make a positive influence on this world on his own. I really want to swoop in and get him off to a great start, but I know he must develop this on his own.

When he was in middle school, I tried, by paying him to read John Maxwell's books. He wanted the money and I was doing my best to plant seeds of success in him. I've seen those early seeds grow and that's incredibly exciting. But, I also want to save him the years of frustration and failure that I faced. Unfortunately, sometimes the best lessons are the ones you learn on your own. There are no shortcuts to discipline.

WARNING—Proud Mom Moment

Paying my son RJ to read those Maxwell books have produced some tangible results. He's been involved in the HOBY LEADERSHIP program in South Carolina for several years. HOBY is a high school leadership program created by actor Hugh O'Brian, who was most known for his starring roles in the ABC Western television series *The Life and Legend of Wyatt Earp* from 1955-1961.

He participated in the three day summer program after his sophomore year and finished second in the state. He received a scholarship to attend the international program in Chicago that summer. He became director of SC HOBY Operations his junior and senior years in high school.

Now a freshman at Clemson University he was just inducted this week into the National Society of Leadership and Success, Sigma Alpha Pi. He's learning discipline on his own now and making progress. I'm so very proud of him and even more excited to see how much further he'll go, if he continues to grow his discipline.

Figuring out what we can teach our children and accepting and letting go of what they'll need to teach themselves has been my most difficult lesson as a parent. It's one I'm still learning. I have to let go and let my son develop his own discipline.

I just feel like the lessons would be easier for him, if he'd learn them from me.

"If I want to be great I have to win the victory over myself...self-discipline." – Harry S. Truman

I Know How this Story Ends

Whether you're a person of faith or not, chances are you've heard the story of David and Goliath. But, have you ever considered this story as an example of strong mental discipline?

In 1 Samuel 17:50 a teenage David runs an errand for his dad and takes some food to his big brothers in the military. When David gets there, he sees the nine foot giant Goliath for the first time and hears him taunting the soldiers.

"I dare you to pick someone to fight me," Goliath said. The soldiers were terrified to fight the behemoth, but not little David. While the fighting men believed Goliath was too big to defeat, David believed Goliath was too big to miss. So he grabbed five small stones and his slingshot and was ready for battle.

David remembered his past successes that had come from his discipline of guarding his sheep all day, every day. He did it in good weather and bad weather and probably on holidays too. He had killed lions and bears with his trusty sling-shot, protecting his wooly four legged friends and he believed the Lord who saved him and his sheep from the wild animals would save him from this giant too.

Mental discipline helped him be brave. It prepared him for battle. My pastor Steven Furtick from Elevation Church recently taught us about this story from a perspective I had never considered before.

It takes mental discipline not to have a bad attitude toward the ordinary. Pastor Steven reminded me that God shows up in the ordinary. I suspect there were days David didn't like watching those sheep or being an errand boy for his brothers, but he kept a good attitude. Bad attitudes can keep us from our destiny by preventing us from developing discipline.

David could have complained to his dad that he didn't want to run an errand. He could have gotten hung up on the attitude his big brother gave him when he saw him, but David chose well. He was focused on the end result. He knew, with God, all things are possible.

"Don't be afraid to give your best to seemingly small jobs. Every time you conquer one, it makes you that much stronger. If you do the little ones well, the big ones tend to take care of themselves." Dale Carnegie

David had the discipline to do the ordinary small things in life well. Every day he guarded his sheep. Can you imagine a more boring task? He sat in the fields and watched for predators, and when they came, he attacked them. I bet he did a lot of push-ups and sit-ups out in the field to pass the time and build up his strength. I like to think he jogged around the sheep for hours to build up endurance. He probably didn't see any direct results of his work, but he did it anyway. His mental discipline prepared him for his big moment with destiny.

I believe David never considered failure as an option the day he went up against Goliath. Yes, he had faith that his GOD would help him, but his discipline gave him confidence as well.

It was as if he knew how the story ended before it began. He was walking in his destiny. He had the discipline and knowledge from the past that he had killed a lion and a bear. This part of the story ends with David hitting Goliath on the forehead and breaking his skull. He didn't have a sword or armor. He did it with the least likely weapon, stones and a slingshot. He had developed discipline and knew how to use that weapon and it paid off for him when he needed it.

I've always seen myself as the underdog. I think that's why I love the story of David and Goliath so much. David was small and the least likely to be famous from his family, but he had a great big heart and was willing to be used to do good in the world. He had the discipline to do the little things with excellence and he had developed the necessary discipline to be ready when opportunity presented itself. Like you and I, he wanted to make a positive impact.

Pastor Furtick reminded us not to say, "I am only..." You fill in your own blank here.

I am only a teenager.

I am only a single mom with no education.

I am only a lonely old man.

It doesn't matter how you fill in the blank. You were created for greatness and my faith has taught me anything is possible. I want to have the discipline in my life to be ready to be used anyway God wants to use me, when he wants to use me.

"We must all suffer one of two things: the pain of discipline or the pain of regret and disappointment." – Jim Rohn

I don't think you want the pain and regret of not developing discipline. You don't want your destiny to pass you by because you ignored the power that comes from doing the ordinary extraordinarily. That doesn't happen without discipline. How can we do greater things, if we can't do the ordinary well?

We've got to put in the work and the tedious hours that grow our discipline muscle whether we see the results or not. Weeks, months and years of that kind of discipline produces results that everybody dreams about, but too few of us exercise the discipline and stand up to the trouble of life to see their dreams become reality.

"Trouble is character development," Pastor Steven said. My life has proved that statement to be true a million times. My belief is that you will see that in your own life and not give up. If you keep working on your discipline with the ordinary things in your life, I know your story will end with you walking into your great destiny too. Let's do it together.

"Success is nothing more than a few simple disciplines, practiced every day." – Jim Rohn

The Discipline of Legends

Aretha Franklin grew up in Detroit and has been called the greatest female artist in Rock-n-Roll history. She was known for working hard. She had discipline. She said, "Great work and great music are the result of creative honesty." Consider Aretha's secret sauce to success. Work honestly, creatively and with discipline.

Growing your discipline comes with time and if I'm being honest, with failure. I still hate that word, but it's necessary for my growth and yours. I don't know of anyone who was able to be an overnight success. We may think that of celebrities, because we don't know their backstory. We all have a backstory.

I've spent 30 years on television. It's flattering when people tell me I seem so natural on TV. It has become easier to just be myself on camera, but it's taken me many years, many mistakes, and the discipline to keep working on getting better to get to that comfortable stage.

I had a talent coach who told me early on that I'd be incredibly successful when I learned how to let the real me show up on TV. I didn't understand what she was saying until years later when I would watch old tapes of myself and die laughing as I tried to be Katie Couric, a beloved NBC Today show host who was at the peak of her career, when I was just starting mine.

It took me at least a decade to figure out who I really was and how I could share that with the people who turned to my channel to watch.

"Respect your efforts, respect yourself. Self-respect leads to self-discipline. When you have both firmly under your belt, that's real power." – Clint Eastwood

Growing up, I loved watching figure skating. The athletes made gliding on the ice look effortless.

I took ice skating in college and quickly learned how tough it was to slide around on a single blade.

As a child, I loved watching Dorothy Hamill. She won the 1976 Olympic gold medal in Austria. She made it look so effortless. She said, "That's what skating is all about; trying to make it look as though it flows." But she didn't win that gold medal without a tremendous amount of discipline.

Countless hours before dawn spent in cold ice rinks on weekends, holidays with what I suspect were very few days off. That daily discipline was her secret to success.

What it boiled down to for Aretha, Dorothy and any other successful person is that they found a way to use their passion combined with the desire for results to help them bond with discipline. It is a critical key to unlock our dreams.

Remember the hardest person you will ever have to lead is yourself. Whether you see yourself as an athlete or not Nike's slogan "*Just Do It*" can help you. Start small and focus on changing one negative characteristic about yourself or choose to develop one new good habit. You can master it in 21 days or it will at least become a little easier to do or not do after three short weeks. Think about it. Your life could be a lot better in less than a month. I know you can commit to that.

Here's a reminder. The devil's in the details. You need to develop the discipline to do the little things before the big things become possible.

I hope you love the David and Goliath story as much as I do. Are you willing to pay the price by doing the little things so that you can walk into your great destiny? If it were easy everyone would do it, but they don't. They live in the land of excuses and procrastination. Nobody sets their GPS for that destination, but so many people end up there. Why? Because they fail to develop the discipline needed to get them where they want to go.

When will you start to develop it? Tomorrow isn't a day of the week. It will never be the right time to start developing discipline, so start developing it NOW.

"Self-discipline is the No.1 delineating factor between the rich, the middle class, and the poor." – Robert Kiyosaki

CHAPTER 6
DEVELOP YOUR STRENGTHS

"Strength and growth come only through continuous effort and struggle." Napoleon Hill

Discovering your strengths isn't as easy as it may sound. Be careful not to confuse strengths with passions. Passion is something that energizes you and you can often lose yourself in it, but that doesn't always mean that's a strength of yours.

Here's an example. You can be passionate about animals, but you may not have the skills, talents or strengths to be a veterinarian.

Once you figure out the difference, you're on your way. If you're good at something, what will it take to get great at it? People don't pay for good, but they'll pay for great.

The answer is usually more practice. Not just doing it more often, but doing it correctly, more often. Poor practice doesn't get you where you want to go.

A negative self image may tell you that you're not good at anything, but I am here to tell you that the negative voice in your head lies like a cheap rug!

To Woo or Not to Woo

Everyone has strengths, many that they may not even realize. There are a lot of online tests you can take to help you discover your strengths. I'm a huge fan of Tom Rath's book, StrengthsFinders 2.0.

When I read it the first time, I didn't realize there were so many different kinds of strengths. Awareness is such a critical part of the process. After you read about the dozens of strengths, you take an online test to discover which are your top five. Here's the really amazing part to me. Over time your strengths can change, which makes it a good idea to go back and take the online survey every so often. I've taken it four times over the last two decades and it's nailed me every time.

To me, the secret of StrengthsFinders is the idea of not wasting time on what you don't do well, and focusing on what you already do at least fairly well.

I'd always been a people person, but I didn't know I had the ability to Woo. What's Woo, you ask?

It's an internal magnet that attracts people to you and it's very valuable in sales, recruiting top talent and selling your ideas to others.

The real question is how do you make your strengths even stronger? Repetition is one way. You've probably heard the phrase practice makes perfect, but you often get better at things through struggles too.

"Strength does not come from winning. Your struggles develop your strengths. When you go through hardships and decide not to surrender, that is strength." —Arnold Schwarzenegger

Pushing yourself to develop your strengths so you can be ALL you were created to be means exploring new possibilities. That frustrating dilemma you've been dealing with can be the key to your destiny.

I'm a learner, that's why I've spent more than 20 years in Public Television leadership. But the key to truly learning is applying what you learn, and for me, that often involves teaching what I learn to others.

Earlier, I told you about the General Manager who gave me my first job in Public Television, James Baum. He was a catalyst for me. He pushed me hard in a million areas of television that I had no experience in like lighting and camera angles. Those were difficult days, but he also spoke success into me.

He said, "One day, Amy, you'll make a great General Manager." That phrase attached itself to my heart and I set out to develop the necessary strengths to make it happen. It was a long and tedious 10 years, before it actually happened. My original strengths were in writing, storytelling and on-camera work, but I learned fundraising, programming, engineering, marketing and operations.

Everything I was learning during those early days, I'd teach my team. My "WOO" strength came in handy in that process, but I worked hard to develop it too. I went to one day seminars, conferences and read every leadership book I could get my hands on. They say teaching helps cement the learning in you and I feel like that's exactly what it did for me.

Once I realized I was pretty darn good at learning, I focused on learning more, which led to strengthening my problem solving skills. It was an output of my ability to learn quickly and learning quickly is a survival skill if you work in non-profit media and most other careers these days.

At first, when James said I would be a great General Manager, I thought he was crazy. Then, I thought he was just being kind. But he planted a seed I had never thought about before. My insatiable desire to read leadership books became the water that helped that seed grow to develop the necessary skills and strengths I needed to build to lead a Public Television station and one day write this book.

The accomplishments of my team and I became the sunshine that fed the sprout of that seed. And together, that little phrase by someone I greatly respected, turned into a dream, which through developing my strengths became my reality.

I have NO DOUBT you have amazing strengths and if you allow yourself to become a bit of a farmer, you will be able to grow them too and your life will be filled with possibilities.

Possibility Thinking

While everybody has different strengths they can develop, I believe there's one strength that everyone can develop.

Hold on, before you dismiss it, I'm not talking about what makes people a great chef, good mechanic or talented engineer. This doesn't require science or math.

I'm talking about helping you develop your strength of becoming a possibility thinker. It will take time, training and discipline, I told you all these D's worked together, but you too can become a possibility thinker.

By focusing on continuous improvement, looking for the positive in everything and considering the possibilities, you too can develop this powerful strength. We often think there's only one way to solve a particular problem, but when you realize there are many ways, it opens up more opportunities for success.

Everyone knows the phrase, "If the door is closed, go through the window." That's the first step of possibility thinking. Realizing there's more than one way to achieve your dreams and if the first, second or even the tenth thing doesn't work, reevaluate, be strategic and try, try again.

"Sometimes you don't realize your own strength until you come face to face with your greatest weakness." Susan Gale

I confess that it's not always easy to help people grow their strengths. It can feel that looking at our weaknesses, or the weaknesses of our team members, is only focusing on the things that are being done wrong. However, sometimes that evaluation is necessary to help people find their destiny. Let's use writing as an example. I told you I'd been a writer since I was in elementary school. I'd always done well on high school writing assignments, but journalistic writing was a whole new thing I needed to learn when I went to college. I wrote for our school's daily newspaper THE BG NEWS. Every day, for an entire semester, news editor Ron Fritz decimated my stories. He rewrote almost everything. I confess to being hurt, discouraged and often felt defeated, but I refused to give up. I decided to focus on the possibility that Ron could teach me a lot, and he did.

Everyone has skills, but sometimes a person's skills aren't in alignment with the skills needed to be successful in their current position. If the leader didn't address the issue, the person would stay frustrated in their current position and never find the job that allowed them to use THEIR STRENGTHS.

Nearly two decades ago, I hired an intern to be a television producer. She was an amazing intern. She had a journalism degree, was always on time, hard working and gave her best every day. She was very organized.

However, she didn't understand that we weren't doing creative writing, where you could make up all the details of a good story. I talked to her about it several times, but she couldn't grasp the concept.

Unfortunately, I had to let her go to find her passion and a job that utilized all of her strengths. I had to give her the freedom to find her great destiny somewhere else.

Years later, she returned for my goodbye party from the Pennsylvania station and told me the day I had to let her go turned out to be one of the best days of her life. She realized she was in the wrong profession before I let her go, but didn't know how to make a change. She kept working on things she wasn't good at and simply got too frustrated to clearly see her options.

She went back to school to be a nurse and was helping people heal. Her compassion and skills made her an extraordinary nurse. Others needed her to walk into her great destiny as a nurse to help them through health problems.

That's a tough situation to be in a job that doesn't match your strengths. Changing jobs is often the best answer, but that can be easier said than done. It takes courage to make a call like that. Everyone has strengths and we all need to find a career that allows us to develop our strengths and that doesn't require us to operate from our weaknesses. While changing our careers can be a tough way to find our strengths, it may be the only options to get to your destiny.

Your Strength Development Toolkit

You may not be Mr. or Ms. Fixit, I'm not either, but we can all appreciate the concept that you need the right tools in your toolbox to put things together. Imagine our strengths need that too. If you use the tools I suggest below, you'll become as powerful at developing your strengths as Tim the Toolman Taylor was at building things, from the popular 90s sitcom *Home Improvement.*

Step one, visualize with me. What color is your toolbox? Any color is fine. Mine is pink and it's a big toolbox, the size the pit crews at NASCAR races would use. Imagining how big it is helps you realize just how much work you have to do.

The first tool that goes inside is practice. It seems so simple doesn't it? Anyone can do it, but fatigue and a lack of discipline get the best of most people. Research shows if you do something 10,000 times you'll be an expert. Honestly, is there anything you've done 10,000 times in your life yet? Most people answer no, but guess what? You still have time. Start practicing or resume practicing now and do it every day. Leadership is one of my strengths and I've read hundreds of books and worked hard to practice the techniques I've learned in each of them.

The next tool we're going to add is a rubber band. Now you think I've completely lost it, but hang in there with me. That rubber band reminds you that you've got to stretch yourself. You know that limp rubber band just sitting there is worthless, but when you stretch it, it finds its destiny. It was meant to be stretched and YOU were too. None of us become who we were created to be without stretching and pulling ourselves outside our comfort zone. They say you never really know how to do something until you teach someone else how to do it.

I've been intentionally teaching people how to grow their strengths for over 20 years and I've become comfortable doing the uncomfortable things. Stretching myself is the way I learn and grow. Even after 30 years in broadcasting, it seems almost every week I find myself stretching to learn and do something I've never done before. How can I do that you might ask? Like anything it gets easier the more you do it. That's the benefit of practice my friends. The rubber band in my toolbox is super stretchy.

Next up, I had to find a mentor to put in my toolbox. Unofficially, I had a lot of them. No one took me under their wing and said, "Amy, let me show you the way." I learned from every boss I had. Some showed me skills I wanted to develop and others taught me how I didn't want to lead, both were critically important. The mentors who influenced me the most were ones I had never met. They were the authors of the books I had read. There are no excuses here. While it's wonderful to have a real human being as your mentor, everyone has the ability to find mentors through reading.

GO FOR IT

The final tool I'd like you to put in your toolbox for now is the swoosh from the NIKE logo. Stay with me here for a minute. This may seem a bit abstract. I'm taking you somewhere important. I promise.

Do you like criticism? I don't know anyone who does. Even so-called constructive criticism is often hard to handle.

But, I want you to imagine that swoosh symbolizes growth and constructive criticism. You can do that right? And can we agree that everyone benefits from growing? I think we can. In order to grow, we often need to hear *how* we can grow.

When coaching people I've always talked with them about their "growth opportunities." Instead of saying, "This is what you're doing wrong," I say, "Here is a **G**rowth **O**pportunity!"

Let's **GO** for your growth opportunity. Just do it. I know you can. And that brings us back to the NIKE swoosh. When you train your brain to hear that people want to help you not hurt you, you will be better prepared to receive their help and advice. It can be your parents, family members, bosses, mentors, or athletic coaches. Actually, everyone in your life that offers advice to help you be all you can be plays a role in you getting to your destiny. You need to be able to receive that advice. I know it's not easy, but if it were easy everyone would be great. You can ride that swoosh all the way to your destiny by focusing on developing your strengths.

Now that toolbox of yours is filled with things that will help you develop your strengths. You'll be faster than Disney's Lightning McQueen in the movie Cars racing in the Piston Cup. See that checkered flag at the finish line my friends, and don't stop until you get there.

"All the adversity I've had in my life, all my troubles and obstacles, have strengthened me.... You may not realize it when it happens, but a kick in the teeth may be the best thing in the world for you." —Walt Disney

CHAPTER 7
DEFEAT DISAPPOINTMENT

What do you do when disappointment comes? When it
weighs on you like a rock, you can either let it press you
down until you become discouraged, even devastated, or
you can use it as a stepping-stone to better things.

Joyce Meyer

Defeating disappointment is always easier said than done,
but it can be done.

When we're disappointed, we sometimes forget that we're
humans and instead think we're pigs. We wallow in the
mud, actually it's our own sadness, because we think it
makes us feel better.

I'm all for venting and talking through our
disappointments, but we must put a limit on it so we can
move forward.

I try my best to nail that coffin of disappointment shut when I go to bed at night.

When I wake up the next day, I force myself to start thinking about solutions. What actions do I need to take to turn around the situation? I work hard to be solution oriented. That's my favorite way to defeat disappointment.

> "Disappointments are just God's way of saying I've got something better. Be Patient. Live Life. Have Faith."
>
> *Lanette Sem*

I find possible solutions so uplifting. I think it has to do with the power that comes over me when I take action. Even if it's not the right solution, the power of taking action seems to create a positive feeling in me and even the wrong action steps usually lead us to the next step that can get us to the desired outcome.

One of the keys to defeating disappointment is to build momentum to get out of the rut. Arriving at possible solutions helps to rock your tires back and forth and before you know it, you are out of the rut and onto real progress.

Romans 8:28 states, "God works all things together for the good of those who love him and are called according to his purpose." In other words, something good can come from the depths of disappointment.

Taking action helps. Give it a try. I bet you'll have the same positive outcome.

I'll try something for a while and if it doesn't work, I'll search for another solution and if that doesn't work, what do you think I do? I know you know the answer to this one. You guessed it. I will try something else.

Some days I call it, "Pitfall Planning." I'm trying to plan my way out of the pit by avoiding it.

Life is filled with choices and we must choose to see the good in everything, even the bad. Bad things can make you stronger...if you allow them to make you better and not bitter.

Disappointment is really just a term for our refusal to look on the bright side.

Richelle E. Goodrich

Bitter Bites

Let's dissect that word for a minute. What does it mean to be bitter? My perspective on bitter means you're angry at the world or angry at the person or situation that caused you pain.

Disappointment can turn to anger and bitterness at the speed of light. Bitterness refuses to acknowledge its rival, sweetness, that which is good in our world. To stay bitter is to keep what is sweet, or what may become sweet down the road, out of the picture. And the co-pilot of bitterness is anger.

I've always said anger is the most worthless emotion. It doesn't hurt the person you're angry with: it only hurts you and chances are you've already endured enough pain from the situation. There are those rare people who use anger to motivate themselves to do better, but more often than not it can eat you alive.

Researchers at the Mayo Clinic have found that bitterness can lead to a slew of problems for you that include:

1. Poor Relationships
2. Mental Health Issues
3. Anxiety
4. Stress
5. Hostility
6. High Blood Pressure
7. Depression
8. Weakened Immune System
9. Heart Problems
10. Poor Self-Esteem

So how do you let go of bitterness? MayoClinic.org shares these tips to help you learn how to forgive.

How do I reach a state of forgiveness?

Forgiveness is a commitment to a personalized process of change. To move from suffering to forgiveness, you might:

- Recognize the value of forgiveness and how it can improve your life
- Identify what needs healing and who needs to be forgiven and for what
- Consider joining a support group or seeing a counselor
- Acknowledge your emotions about the harm done to you and how they affect your behavior, and work to release them
- Choose to forgive the person who's offended you
- Move away from your role as victim and release the control and power the offending person and situation have had in your life

I have another philosophy that may help you defeat disappointment. I say this a lot.

Choose joy.

Let go of the myth that you should always be happy. Happiness is an emotion that's contingent upon things that happen to you, things that you often have no control over, like the weather, someone else's attitude, the day of the week, or someone on social media who seems to be having a better day than you.

I have a little red glitter Christmas ornament that sits on my desk all year long that says JOY as a reminder that joy is a choice. I choose joy and I hope you will too. It can help you defeat disappointment and gain perspective.

When you realize you have the power to choose and take action to make your destiny a reality, your focus shifts.

In 2008, I felt I was getting close to making my dream come true of becoming a PBS General Manager. That's when my professional life was rocked. A work issue, like I had never endured before, hit me upside the head like a cast iron skillet.

My integrity was questioned professionally and my reputation was severely damaged and I knew I hadn't done anything wrong. I thought I was going to lose my job. These were some of the darkest weeks of my life and it stretched over several months.

I called a friend and prayer warrior, Curtissa Odi, and told her what was going on and she reminded me that it's not over until God says it's over. Those words have helped me defeat disappointment many times over the years.

I bet you have one of those positive friends in your life too. Maybe it's a family member who no matter what's happening in your life, they help you feel better. Don't be afraid to ask for their help.

> **We must accept finite disappointment, but never lose infinite hope.**
>
> *Martin Luther King, Jr.*

Learn to Let it Go

During that time, I had to drag myself out of bed every morning and go to work, which had never been the case before. I loved what I did, and knew I was lucky to spend my life doing what I was passionate about, creating meaningful television content. However, the issue I was involved in was all consuming.

It was all I could think about, but I was still a wife and a mother of an eight-year-old at the time. I could not afford to keep myself mired in this disappointment.

As I mentioned earlier, I'm a person of faith and one day, praying and crying in my car on my way to work, God brought to my mind the verse, "Be still and know that I am God." That's from Psalm 46:10.

For folks who may not share my same faith, I would urge you to listen to that soft voice in your head. The loud voices of doubt need no amplifier. But those soft voices of calm, of support and of peace, often need the volume turned up. In times of disappointment and stress, listen closely to those soft voices.

Being still didn't make an ounce of sense to me. I was working so hard trying to figure out what I was going to do to fix the problem. I wanted to know what action I could take to make things better. I had always been proud of being a person of action.

I was convinced this was the exact wrong time that I was supposed to be still. It sounded absolutely crazy to me.

But I soon realized that Elsa in Disney's movie Frozen actually knew what she was singing about in the song, "Let it Go." I had to let it go and let GOD fix this one. I knew he could, but I confess to being nervous that he wouldn't.

The person who had treated me so horribly didn't seem to care and I was somehow just supposed to "be still."

After several months, the person admitted to thinking I had done something inappropriate behind her back, but learned it was someone else and not me. One of the shocking things about disappointment is sometimes it can disappear as quickly as it appeared, but sometimes it doesn't.

One of the hardest things I EVER had to do was learn how to pray for my enemies. Those prayers helped me get over that awful situation. I had to feel sorry for the person who was mean to me, lied about me in order to defeat my own disappointment.

Doing nothing but praying for the person who hurt me and having faith that things would get better was actually the greatest action I could take.

Again, for those with a different faith path than mine, think about what happens when you pity the person who is causing you pain. By taking the higher ground, you gain the advantage for yourself. You bring yourself a peace of mind that no one can take away.

Whether it is through prayer or pity or simple meditation, getting yourself above the fray is about protecting yourself and moving you forward. It may seem like you are letting the other party off the hook, but to the contrary, you are propelling yourself toward success by releasing anger and bitterness.

Here's another Maxwell quote that has made a major impact on my life. "Hurting people, hurt people." Just understanding what that truly means helps me have compassion on the other person and actually enables me to pray for them. I confess it's still not easy to pray for people who don't treat me the way I'd like to be treated, but those prayers free me from anger and resentment. It's actually a benefit for me as well as them.

As difficult as that test was, the challenge with life is that the tests get harder. I have failed tests many times before passing them. If I thought this disappointment journey was hard, I was about to realize that the next two disappointment tests I was to encounter were going to be exponentially more difficult.

> **One's best success comes after their greatest disappointments.**
>
> *Henry Ward Beecher*

Things settled down for a couple years and then another test hit me. This time it was personal, not professional. My husband of 19 years, who handled the checkbook, admitted to me that we were $50,000 in debt.

He'd never mentioned a word about even being a few thousand dollars behind. I thought we had been paying ahead on our house and saving money for our son's college and that my husband and best friend had it all under control.

His explanation was that we had just been overspending, because we'd been saving so much. I didn't really believe him. I thought he was cheating on me or gambling.

I developed what felt like the world's worst headache. It lasted weeks. I went to the doctor, who said there wasn't anything wrong with me physically, but my world was rocked.

I thought my marriage was over. He had been my very best friend for over 20 years. When you lose trust in someone, it takes a long time to regain it.

I relied on my faith to get us through that difficult time and God did a miracle in our finances that allowed us to pay off that debt in just about two-and-a-half years, but now I needed God to do a miracle in my heart and help me forgive Rob.

I wrote about bitterness earlier in this chapter. It was eating me alive and I had to choose to forgive him. Once I let go of my own stubbornness and the grudge that I was holding, it seemed like forgiveness came instantly. Ok, let's be real, it actually took about three years before I could truly let it go. While I learned to let it go, the more difficult part was forgetting it.

It didn't seem possible, but with God ALL THINGS ARE POSSIBLE. That's the motto of the state of Ohio, where I was born, based on Matthew 19:26.

We cut back on everything and really tightened our purse strings. Calling it a disappointing time doesn't adequately paint the picture, but defeating that disappointment was another critical part of my life and helped prepare me for what was ahead.

> **Disappointments are to the soul what a thunderstorm is to the air.**
>
> *Friedrich Schiller*

The next traumatic milestone of defeating disappointment in my life lasted about four years from March 2012 through June 2016. In March of 2012, I was still at the Public Television station in Bethlehem, Pennsylvania.

About 10 years had passed since my former boss James had told me I'd make a great GM one day.

A leadership change happened at the station and I thought this was the day I had been waiting patiently for, but it wasn't. After being at the station since I was 31 and now at 44, I realized that if I wanted to lead a station, it was going to be somewhere else.

My heart was broken. I didn't want to uproot my family, leave our friends, our church and a community I had fallen in love with over the last 18 years, but a leader must lead.

I often turn to reading to help me get through difficult times. A fellow John Maxwell Team member Lisa Brouwer from South Dakota suggested I read Mark Batterson's book "Circle Maker." It talked about praying circles around your problems...literally walking around the physical issue every day for seven days. So I did.

I got up early every morning for a week in January and walked around my Pennsylvania office building in the frigid temperatures. At the beginning of the week, I prayed to be the CEO there, but something changed over the days and my prayers changed to I want to lead wherever you want me GOD. I'll go wherever you take me, just help me to know your plan.

My heart's desires had changed in that short time. It's hard to explain, but suddenly I had surrendered my desires for God's plan. Trust me, that's always a better choice, but it's rarely an easy one to make.

"Circle Maker" was a catalyst to help me defeat disappointment and take the next step toward my destiny. I highly recommend reading it for yourself.

Be Careful What you Wish For

A few months later, I became the General Manager at PBS Charlotte in North Carolina.

My husband was excited to leave the frigid weather of Pennsylvania behind for the sunny south and his sister lived nearby. Sounds like the perfect ending, right? Not exactly.

Our 12-year-old son was devastated when we told him about the move and I felt like the worst mom on Earth. But I knew he would make new friends and I felt at peace with the decision. I believed this was part of our collective destiny.

When I got to Charlotte's beautiful skyline, I had tremendous excitement about this new opportunity, but reality settled in immediately.

The station almost closed its doors in 2012 and it had few resources remaining. It was $1.3 million in debt and it was my job to fix everything and to pay back the money that had been lost.

No problem, I thought. I'd overcome adversity before. I'd fixed a deficit before. I believed God brought me here, and since he'd brought me this far, I didn't think he'd leave me now. My faith is what got me through three incredibly challenging, personally painful years, so why wouldn't that be exactly what I needed now? It was, but I had to start looking at faith a bit differently.

These days, I had to look at life as what God could do through me. He was using me to do something that I would never dream of taking credit. It seemed impossible, but that's God's speciality. He delights in using people to make his plans come true. When the change is so big, we mere mortals can't take credit for it.

That's exactly what God did through me at PBS Charlotte, but it took a lot longer than I had hoped.

Two months after I arrived, we were off the air for three days during a major fundraising drive. A PBS station can't make money if people can't watch.

The roof of the station leaked and if that were not enough, there were plenty of personnel challenges to overcome.

We had very few corporate donors, very few individual donors and not many viewers.

That first year, I grappled with what often felt like depression, but I refused to accept it. I couldn't wait to go to sleep at night, so the day would be over. I was physically and emotionally exhausted.

Every morning, by God's grace, I had hope that things would get better. Failure wasn't an option. We made great progress during my first two years, but it never felt like enough. There were always hundreds of other things that needed to be fixed.

I had to sing songs I learned as a child in Sunday school to keep myself going.

You may know this one, "If you want joy, you must ask for it. If you want you, you must ask for it. The joy of the Lord is my strength." I had to make the choice to sing about joy, when I couldn't feel an ounce of joy.

Singing that song, usually just in my mind, gave me strength to push through those dark, very dark, days.

The change I wanted to see didn't happen overnight. It took months.

But that act of singing about the joy that I didn't have allowed me to tap into the joy that came directly from God. I'm so very grateful that my creator cared enough to allow me to borrow HIS joy until I could develop my own.

You can develop that same joy by focusing on the positive and expressing gratitude. Here's an exercise that can help. Get an empty jar or can and write down things that you're grateful for every day on small pieces of paper and put them inside. Be consistent and do it for a whole year. Then, on December 31st dump them out and read them all to be reminded of what "A WONDERFUL LIFE," you have. The key is focusing on the positive.

Fast forward to today, and I'm grateful to say I just wrapped up landing our sixth consecutive cash positive budget and in six years we've paid back all but more than $100,000 in debt. We've won four regional Emmys and grown viewers and donors in a way a station our size shouldn't be able to do but we did.

Our success happened, in part, because I believed it could, even though the reality around me often made it seem impossible. Our team worked hard and made great progress. Through prayer, positive thinking, reading and focusing on my growth and the growth of our team, we did it together.

We turned the Titanic around and avoided the iceberg. Now that's defeating disappointment.

Has it been easy? No!!!! Has it been rewarding? Absolutely! Have I had plenty of opportunities to perfect my problem solving skills and defeat disappointment over and over again? You betcha!

Moving forward frees you to stop looking over your shoulder at the past and helps you focus on the future. You can't always control what happens, but you have control over how you react to what life sends your way.

No one else has that power over you, unless you give it to them. You get to decide.

Will you take control and actively defeat disappointment? Or will you give control to someone else by holding on to your hurt?

I'm here to encourage you to take your life back and work toward making it what you've always dreamed, no matter what heart breaking things have happened to you.

Let's take a second here. You may be thinking that this is easier said than done. Perhaps you think your disappointment is deeper than anyone can imagine. A past that included abuse, being unemployed, a cancer diagnosis, some other life changing disappointment that no one else can fathom.

Those things that happen to you do not define you, unless you give them the power by staying bitter. They may be the only thing you focus on today, but they're not your destiny.

I believe our experiences dealing with our current challenges is exactly what we need in order to help others get through challenges of their own in the future. It makes us relatable. It gives us a connection we wouldn't have otherwise.

How many people can trace their own success in defeating a problem to the assistance of someone who only knew what to do because they had that same problem? Your current disappointment may be the very ticket to your ability to help someone else in the future.

"Anytime you suffer a setback or disappointment, put your head down and plow ahead."

Les Brown

No Pity Parties

Take Wilma Rudolph, for example. She contracted polio and had to wear a brace to help her walk. That sounds like a fair reason to live life in a personal pity party, don't you think? Wilma didn't.

Wilma was the 20th of 22 children. Just five years after taking off her braces, this determined athlete won a bronze medal for sprinting at the 1956 Olympics. You must persevere to win no matter how difficult your disappointment.

The Worry Trap

"Worry never robs tomorrow of its sorrow, it only saps today of its joy."
– Leo F. Buscaglia

Often when we're disappointed about something, we can start to worry. Thoughts like, "Will it ever get better?" or "How can I get past this?" can dominate our minds.

I admit, it's not easy to avoid those questions and avoid worrying.

No matter what has happened, a failed test, a lost job or a concerning report from the doctor, as humans, it's tough not to worry.

It's easy to make the problems in our lives enormous in our imagination and just as easy to minimize the things that are going well.

But the key is to remain grateful for all that you have going right and understand that what is going wrong or disappointing you is going to make you stronger.

Practice an attitude of gratitude. That's an action we're all capable of. Expressing gratitude for other things in your life that are working well can change your attitude and perspective about the thing that is disappointing you.

Don't let yourself believe that there's nothing to be grateful for, because there's always something. If you're disappointed about finances, be grateful for your health. If you're dealing with a health issue, be grateful you have a home to heal in. Did you wake up today in a warm house in peacetime? You have more things going for you than you thought!

Recently, Pastor Steven Furtick said, "When God does new things, it often looks like trouble," which is usually why we're disappointed, but it's just training."

I've had lots of that training in my life and this is why age is such a wonderful thing. When trouble finds me now, I don't freak out half as much as I did when I was younger.

I'm not perfect at it, but I've learned how to let go and let God do his part, at least most of the time. He always shows up and he always does a better job than I ever could. However, he rarely does it the way I would have done it or as quickly as I would like. That's something I am working on myself.

Your Super Power

One of the first famous comediennes, Lucille Ball once said, "Luck? I don't know anything about luck. I've never banked on it and I'm afraid of people who do. Luck to me is something else: hard work...and realizing what is opportunity and what isn't."

That's great advice, but why is it so darn hard to put into action?

Make ACTION your superpower. It's better than leaping a tall building in a single bound.

Action can be addicting, in a good way. The more you do, the more you can get done and the more you'll want to do.

This may sound too simple to actually work, but it does.

The greatest method of defeating disappointment is deciding that you will get through this, no matter what. Very few things, with the exception of death, are actually final.

You can find a new job. You can rebuild your life. You can help your teenager learn to make better choices.

You are far more resilient than you think.

When I was younger and newly married, I often felt like life was over when things didn't work out the way I had hoped.

As a young television reporter and anchor, I heard it all. I didn't get dozens of jobs I thought I wanted.

My husband Rob, a very laid back man, used to say, "Will the sun rise tomorrow?" I'd say yes, and he'd follow up with, "Then you get another chance to solve it."

At first, that advice made me a little angry. Didn't he realize how distraught I was over the issue or how disappointed I was?

However, age and experience taught me he was a GENIUS when he offered that advice. We high strung, over achievers, need people who bring calm to our lives.

I'm afraid I've never thanked him for teaching me that so I want to do it publicly here.

Dear Rob,

Your support and encouragement, through both good times and bad, over nearly three decades, has allowed me to fly higher than I ever thought possible and I feel like I've only just begun.

You were the answer to a teenage girl's prayers. I asked God to give me a husband who would always love me, just for me, exactly as I was, and I'm so very grateful he gave me you.

Thank you for being my everlasting secret weapon to defeating disappointment!

Love,
Amy

Now, that doesn't mean being married to your exact opposite is easy. It isn't, but it's exactly what GOD knew I needed and I'm grateful, even when I want to strangle him.

Here we are wrapping up another chapter packed full of options to help you defeat disappointment. Seeking solutions goes hand-in-hand with making action your superpower. Believe you can leap over that disappointment in a single bound and you will.

You have everything you need inside of you to do it, but if you're feeling extra blue some days, don't be afraid to reach out to an encouraging friend or family member. That's why they're in your life, to help you see that you can get past anything and everything in life with a big dose of encouragement.

Remember to avoid bitterness, your health depends on it. When you let go of that bitterness you might as well practice forgiveness. Forgiving people will allow you to

end your personal pity party and can help you stop
worrying too.

Finally, let go of the myth that you have to always feel
happy. There will be days that you just won't be happy and
that's when you need to remind yourself to choose joy.
Get yourself one of those glittery ornaments as a reminder.

**"Disappointment is just the action of your brain
readjusting itself to reality after discovering things are
not the way you thought they were."**

- Brad Warner

CHAPTER 8
YOUR DESTINY IS CALLING

"It is not in the stars to hold our destiny, but in ourselves." -William Shakespeare

What is your calling, your true destiny? What are you uniquely created to do?

Each of us was put on this earth for a purpose. We have an assignment.

So, how do you figure out what your assignment is?

Tapping into your faith is a great place to start. See what God wants to do through you.

But regardless of your faith, or lack thereof, there is a way to figure out your destiny. You can pick up a book and start reading.

You may have heard of Jack Canfield. He's the creator of the book "Chicken Soup for Your Soul," which turned into a wildly popular franchise of books. He has these 10 tips to help you find your life's purpose.

1. Explore the things you love to do and what comes easy to you.
2. Ask yourself what qualities you enjoy expressing the most in the world.
3. Create a life purpose statement. (That's the mission statement I suggested earlier in this book.)
4. What is your heart telling you? Follow it.
5. Continuously think about where you want to be.
6. Conduct a Passion Test developed by Chris and Janet Attwood. It's pretty simple and powerful. Fill in the blank 15 times for the following statement: "When my life is ideal, I am _____." Make sure you use a verb. For example, one of mine is "When my life is ideal, I am helping others find their destiny."
7. Think about the times you experienced the greatest joy in your life.
8. Answer the question, "When have I felt the most fulfilled?"
9. Align your goals with your purpose and passion.
10. Lean into your life purpose bit by bit.

"You have the power to achieve greatness and create anything you want in life-but you must take action!"
Jack Canfield

It doesn't matter how young or how old you are. What matters is your motive. Why do you want it?

Is it all about you? Start looking at the dreams deep inside of you that just won't go away as a catalyst to help others.

There's nothing wrong with wanting to provide your family a better life. However, you need to be careful not to fall into the trap of bigger, better and more.

John Maxwell taught me through his books that finding your purpose was at the intersection of what you're good at and what you're passionate about.

I use John's book, "Putting Your Dream to the Test," to help my inner city high school students gain the skills to evaluate their dreams.

Here's another reason to push through to find your destiny. Please consider that others *need* YOU to make your dreams come true so they can make their dreams come true. You might be thinking that nobody needs you. Well, think again.

If you want to be a mechanic, millions of people like me need you to be successful. I can't do anything for my car beyond putting gas in it. One of my 3D students, Mario, who made some mistakes and wore an ankle bracelet that meant he was on house arrest during my class, dreams of being an auto mechanic. I told him many times that I needed him to make his dream come true.

Another one of my 3D friends is Dilcia. She dreams of being the best heart surgeon in the world so she can go back to her home country and help provide care in her tiny Mexican village that still doesn't have any doctors. Countless people need her to make her dream come true.

And then there's Marcus. He's so excited about making his dream his reality. He made some mistakes along the way too and spent some time behind bars.

But now he's taking classes at Central Piedmont Community College, enrolled in the heating and cooling program. He wants to build a company that employs first time offenders to be electricians, because he knows how hard it is to get a break after making a mistake.

Marcus, I'm cheering you on and can't wait to see you make your dream come true. Remember, others are counting on you to help them make their dreams come true.

I have one last story for you. Honestly, I'd like to tell you about hundreds of my students, because each and every one of them is special and has an amazing dream, but Allison has a presence that I want to tell you about.

When she stepped in front of our TV cameras to record her "I have a dream" speech, it was electrifying. The camera loved her.

She dreams of being an actress. She realizes the road to making her dream come true won't be easy, but she wants to help others feel joy through her acting and everyone in the world can use a little more joy, don't you think? Two weeks after she graduated from the class she sent me this email.

Hello Ms. Amy!

It's Alli from the 3D project. I am just reaching out to you to tell you that your words of encouragement during the 3D project pushed me to take TWO leaps of faith since then! One leap I took was auditioning for the American Musical and Dramatic Academy! Not only did I get into the school, but I was also offered a $6,000 scholarship! It's not much, but it's something. Another leap of faith I took was signing up for the draft to perform for open mic night at a nearby theater! What you spoke on about fear during the 3D project made me realize how vital it is to step out and do things like this. How important it is to know that the things we freak out about are never as bad as we picture them. Speaking of which, I sent a message to a friend today that said exactly that, which is what made me think of you! I just wanted to say thank you, again, for all the wisdom you poured into me during the 3D project. I thought it would be nice to update you on how you have impacted me.

Sincerely,
Alli

Dear sweet, talented Alli, you have impacted me too by affirming that my dream to add value to others makes a positive impact. You needed me to sow that desire to find your destiny into you and you are already applying what you learned to benefit not only your own life, but your friends' lives as well. Thank you!!

My friends, that's what it's all about.

"It is a mistake to look too far ahead. Only one link of the chain of destiny can be handled at a time." Winston Churchill

I want to make sure you understand what I'm saying that the world needs you to make your dreams come true. It will be a journey and it will probably take close to a lifetime to reach your true destiny. But every step you take is a critical one that is getting you closer and closer to it. So keep moving forward. Keep trying.

Here are a few more examples of clues that can lead you to your destiny.

If you love helping people and want to go into healthcare, millions of people need you to be the very best at it, so when they come to you scared and ill, you can help them.

Do you like to eat? I do, and I'm grateful for all those under appreciated farmers in the world. Where would we be without them?

Do you like your house? We'd all be homeless without builders. How about your air conditioning? As I write this in my cool, comfortable home in South Carolina in July, I am grateful for the HVAC professional that keeps our system running well.

I'm also quite fond of plumbers and electricians. I don't like the dark or clogged pipes.

And where would we be without truck drivers? Store shelves would be empty. Amazon couldn't ship you your purchase, if they didn't have the product on their shelves or someone to get it to you. God bless those wonderful truck drivers.

I can't leave out my gratitude for all the men and women in the U.S. who choose to put their own lives on the line to give me freedom by serving in the military. They are truly walking in their great destinies that give the rest of us opportunities for freedom.

Now you may be thinking, "Amy, why did you mention those jobs and not lawyers, doctors and other highly regarded careers?" Dear friends, you answered that question for yourself. Everyone considers those careers great, but unfortunately our world seems to take for granted jobs like I listed above that truly make our country run. The ones I mentioned don't necessarily require a four year degree, but often pay more than careers that do.

We're All Leaders

You don't have to be famous or a millionaire to be great. Every one of us plays an important role in this world. We are all leaders.

Perhaps you don't see yourself as a leader. I'd ask you to think again.

According to John Maxwell, leadership is influence over others, nothing more, nothing less.

Each of us has influence over someone and usually there are many people we influence each and every day.

At the top of the list are our families. Your kids need to see you walk into your destiny so they can walk into their own.

We aren't in a dress rehearsal. This is the only life you and I have and we must walk into our great destinies so others can walk into theirs. Each of us was created for a great destiny. Do you believe me yet?

"This generation of Americans has a rendezvous with destiny." Franklin D. Roosevelt

"We share one heart, one home, and one glorious destiny." Donald Trump

"Control your own destiny! Control your own destiny!" Stephen Curry

"I've got the ability to control my destiny, and I take pride in that." Jordan Burroughs

Let's circle back and allow these 7 D's to truly sink into you at your core with a quick recap.

1. **Desire Defines Your Dream:** Spend some time really thinking about what you feel called to accomplish. What haven't you been able to shake over the last few years or perhaps your entire life? Are you being pulled in a different direction than

your current situation? Identify it and you're on your way. This desire fuels your dream and will push you through the difficult times.

Don't forget my steps to help you dream again. Love yourself, listen to your inner voice and get excited about learning again. I saved the most important step for last.

You need to write your own personal mission statement to help define your why. When you know your why, everything else starts to line up.

Remember your why needs to be about more than just you. Who will benefit beyond you and your family from you achieving your dreams and walking in your destiny? When you realize others need you to make your dreams come true so they can make their dreams come true, you won't be able to stop until you get there.

2. **Discover Your Passion:** Research shows 74 percent of Americans quit their job to pursue their passion. Passion changes things and it works in tandem with desire.

So many people I meet can't explain what they're passionate about. Keep trying new things until you find the thing that ignites your passion. We often take things for granted or consider them just a hobby. In some cases, they are hobbies at least for now, but what would happen if you poured your heart and soul into that hobby?

What if you took a business class at your local community college or went to your area's small business administration and got free help to actually write a business plan? Develop a list of revenue generating opportunities and create a marketing strategy to actually get paid for doing what you're passionate about.

Sometimes you find your passion through your problems. If I hadn't had staff challenges at my first PBS job, I never would have attended that workshop on how to deal with difficult people and that's where I found my first John Maxwell book that unlocked my passion to grow myself and others to be all we were created to be.

Ask the people who know you best to help you uncover your greatest talents. Passion is usually nearby.

3. **Demolish Negative Thinking:** It's going to take time, but you can change, if you want to. Wanting to is the key ingredient to changing your thought process and becoming more of a possibility thinker. Negativity isn't attractive and it may be the stumbling block preventing you from walking into your great destiny.

You don't want to miss out on the health benefits of positive thinking, because you will live longer and have better coping skills just to name two of them. People are drawn to positivity. You may not even realize you're being negative, but once you become aware, you can squash that worthless habit in about three weeks.

Don't forget about my four steps to undo negative thinking.

1. Practice saying nice things about yourself.

2. Look back at your life and consider all the things you've overcome.

3. Stop saying negative absolutes about yourself like I'll NEVER or NOBODY is as stupid as I am.

4. Put a rubber band around your wrist and flick it every time you have a negative thought or say something negative. Remember, if you have a little relapse, everyone does, breakout another rubber band and repeat the process.

4. **Defer Your Need to Know How:** It's so easy to say I can't do something because I don't know how. It's a crutch you should throw away right now. You don't need it anymore. Here's a little reminder, excuses are worthless. They don't help you be who you want to be and they actually prevent you from getting where you want to go.

Take a step in any new direction. One of two things will happen. It will either lead you to your next step or you'll figure out that wasn't the right step and you'll go in a different direction.

Here's my absolute favorite. Take an inventory of your life and see how many times you successfully did things without knowing how. Sure, it may have taken you a little while, but you did it. Remember those successes!

See your dreams as the rings on a bullseye. Take aim and throw the dart. When you hit anywhere, just adjust and take another throw. Each time you get closer, celebrate, because you're learning how to defer your need to know how.

You figured it out...Congratulations!

5. **Develop Discipline:** Nobody I know likes discipline, from the baby being told "NO" to the overweight adult who doesn't want to eat right and exercise. But remember, discipline is like a muscle. It needs training. The more you develop it, the easier and more impactful it becomes. Seeing results will encourage you to continue to cultivate it, but don't forget to celebrate those little positive results. The joy that comes from recognizing you're making progress helps you push through the often painful process.

David didn't just wake up one morning and kill the giant Goliath. He had been training for years. He had killed the bear and the lion before he ever met Goliath, thanks to developing discipline and confidence.

Once you grow your discipline muscle, there's no stopping what you can accomplish, both personally and professionally. Develop the discipline of legends like Aretha Franklin and Dorothy Hamill. Don't wait until tomorrow to start. Tomorrow isn't a day of the week and tomorrow never comes. Do it NOW.

6. **Discover Your Strengths:** You may be aware of one or two of your strengths, but chances are you have even more. They're often hiding just under the surface and you may be taking them for granted. Take a personality assessment or read a book about strengths. I recommend Tom Rath's Strengthsfinders 2.0. There are so many free online or low cost options that can help you tap into the power that comes from knowing your strengths and it's always a good idea to develop some new ones. It feels great.

Don't waste time on your weaknesses. However, be careful not to be too quick to write things off as weaknesses. Some things that may look like a weakness can be a hidden strength that needs conditioning. You can get better at some things. My favorite example is the fact that while I'm not great at math, I handle a budget like a pro. This is where being poor right out of college turned out to be an asset. I learned how to do a lot with a little and trust me, that skill that was built over time and through difficult circumstances has served me incredibly well over the years. Load up your strength development toolbox with practice, rubber bands, mentors and that Nike swoosh to remind you to "Just Do It."

7. **Defeat Disappointment:**From my perspective, this is one of the harder D's to slay. That's why I made it last, because if you develop the others, they will help give you the encouragement to once and for all bury those disappointments that have been controlling you for too long. They've been preventing you from walking into your great destiny, from fulfilling your purpose in life. I'm not saying don't acknowledge them, just don't let them control you any longer.

Give some thought to how you can use those disappointments to help someone else. There's real power in that. Taking the focus off of yourself and channeling your energy to help someone else get through a similar difficult time is a very valuable journey.

Taking action also helps. The action of choosing to be better and not bitter goes a long way. Choose joy in your life. See the glass as half full, not half empty. You don't have to be a rocket scientist or have a Ph.D to do that. Anyone can choose to see the good even in negative situations. It just takes training.

Finally be like Elsa in Disney's Frozen and "Let it Go!"

There you have it my friends. The seven D's to your destiny, a roadmap to help you fulfill your life's purpose. What could be better than that? You've got this.

There are so many people out there counting on you to make your dreams come true. My biggest worry in life is not accomplishing my God given purpose. I've often called that the greatest failure. It's my greatest desire to be all I was created to be and it can be yours too.

If you're looking for a community of encouragers, come over to my closed Facebook page The 7 D's to Your Destiny. It's no fun to try and make big things happen alone. Share your successes and failures there. I think you'll be encouraged by the stories you see others share.

We all need support and encouragement and giving encouragement is one of the things I was created for. I look forward to seeing you there and I can't wait to hear how you made your dreams come true. I hope this book helps you make it happen.

I'll wrap things up with how I end every 3D course I teach.

Repeat after me. I'm serious, please say this out loud. Every time I say these sentences, I get an extra burst of motivation and encouragement and I believe you will too.

"I have been created for greatness... but the journey will be difficult.

I will fight for my dream.

I will not stop... until I make it my reality.

I am smart enough.

I am capable.

I can do it.

Others need me to make my dream come true.

I won't let a difficult road....

Prevent me from ....

Walking into my great destiny."

How did it feel? I hope you felt empowered. Your final assignment is to say that statement out loud, twice a day for at least 21 days so that it really sinks into your soul. Whenever you feel a little discouraged pull this out and repeat it. Write it on your bathroom mirror or put it on your refrigerator.

Ring Ring...do you hear that? Go ahead and answer it. It's your destiny calling.

ABOUT THE AUTHOR

Amy Burkett grew up in the small town of Uhrichsville, Ohio. Most of her friends stayed in the great Buckeye state, but Amy dared to explore what life could be like outside her comfort zone.

She became a possibility thinker, developed a growth mindset and went on to do things she never dreamed possible. She has led teams to 10 regional Emmy Awards in Philadelphia and Nashville. She took over the helm of a failed PBS station in Charlotte, North Carolina and has led its renaissance, paying back a million dollars in debt, growing community impact, audience, donors and stakeholders since 2013.

Her faith has been her North Star and her love of learning has equipped her to share what she's discovered over a lifetime in this book to help YOU develop the 7D's to Your Destiny.

Amy holds a bachelor's of science in journalism from Bowling Green state University in Ohio and is a certified trainer, speaker and coach with the John Maxwell Team. She lives in the Charlotte area with her husband Rob and their son RJ.

Made in the USA
Columbia, SC
12 September 2020

18515254R00087